THE GERIATRIC GARDENER

Adaptive gardening advice for seniors

By Duane Pancoast

MARK~

THANKS FOR
ATTENDING THE
BOOK PARTY!

SAFE & FUN
GARDENING.

Drew Brent

TABLE OF CONTENTS

How To Adapt

Making Tough Decisions

Making Less Difficult Decisions

Senior Gardening Through the Seasons

When Outdoor Gardening Is Out Of The Question

INTRODUCTION

This barnwood sign was an 80th birthday gift.

Welcome! This book is compiled from posts to a blog called The Geriatric Gardener, which I've written since 2017. Everything you will read here is author tested. Everyone is going to get old. Some of us accept it gracefully while others resist the limitations age places on us. I'm one of the latter.

Now, with a couple of bad knees and a face full of liquid nitrogen every time I go to the dermatologist, I would like to share my experiences so you may recognize the signs of old age. It's said that forewarned is forearmed. I'm the messenger who is forewarning you.

Each chapter contans a new discovery in the aging process and how other aging gardeners and I have either circumvented or learned to live with these limitations. Some of the inspiration came from a book entitled, *Gardening for a Lifetime, How to Garden Wiser as You Grow Older*, by the late Sydney Eddison. Also, landscape industry trade magazines are starting to recognize the need to educate landscape contractors on the needs of older people.

As I've read the little blurb about alumni accomplishments at the back of my college alumni magazine, I've watched my class rise from the very bottom to the years right near the top. I remember commenting to my late wife, "Look at these people from the 1920s and '30s. They're really old." I wonder if new graduates will look at their first issue and say the same thing about my class (1961)?

ATTITUDE IS EVERYTHING

Aging is a fact of life. You can't change it. You can't fight it…and win. You just have to adapt. I know. I've been there, kicking and screaming all the way. I had to finally give in and adapt if I wanted to continue enjoying the landscape that has been my pride and joy over the past decade and a half.

It has taken me a long time to embrace this fact of life. That's why it has taken me so long to write this book. When you've spent your life helping people, it's tough to then have to ask them for help. Having finally raised the white flag, I'm now equipped with my AARP card, Medicare card, handicap parking permit and even a medical alert but am not fully into the senior lifestyle.

When it comes to gardening, I'm fully into the senior scene. It's either adapt or suffer the consequences. And those consequences can be deadly. Carrying cards that identify you as a senior takes no effort and actually has some perks. Getting a head start on adaptive gardening may save you money, as well as your life.

Regardless of your age, when you start thinking about modifying the layout of your garden, redo the paths as well. Replace steps with gentle inclines. Remove rough, uneven pavement and replace it with a smooth but non-slippery surface. Also, light your garden well to show it off, even at night, and to prevent accidents as you age. Making these modifications now can save you money later, as prices continue to rise.

Be sure to design conveniently placed shady spots where you can sit, rest and enjoy a cool drink of water on hot summer days. Frequent hydration breaks are necessary regardless of your age You have to take them more often when you get older. Pacing yourself and maintaining your fluid level may extend the time you can garden before having to take more drastic adaptive measures.

Many of us were taught from childhood that we can do anything we set our minds to. That has shaped our lives but, as we age, our minds and bodies aren't always in agreement. That doesn't mean it's time to give up. It means it's time to adapt; to bring your mind and body back into sync.

You can keep the aging process from redefining you and taking away the pleasures of life. It's all a matter of adapting your attitude to consider your physical limitations and adapting new methods and techniques to your new lifestyle.

Gardening is good, healthy exercise. But let's face it; it's also hard work that, over the years, takes a toll on our bodies. Gardening requires kneeling to reach plants. When younger, you might think that, when your knees wear out, all you have to do is have replacement surgery, and become the bionic gardener. The fact is, your kneeling days will be over... with your worn out natural knees or your mechanical knees. If you accept this early, you may be able to extend your knees' useful life by padding them when gardening. Use one of the seating products on the market or transition to raised or vertical beds.

Gardeners have an independent attitude. There comes a time, though, when you can accept offers of help or reject them and let your physical condition limit your gardening. As time goes on, you'll have to make the decision of whether to seek help or give up gardening altogether. Isn't seeking help the better alternative?

With a positive attitude, you can continue gardening throughout your lifetime. When the time comes to turn over most of your gardening to your helpers, you can still help by making your wishes known to your helpers, while confining your dirty hands to raising houseplants. Nothing wrong with that. Houseplants are the fastest growing segment of the nursery industry, so raising them can't be limited just to seniors. If houseplant care becomes difficult, raising Tillandsia (air plants) is fun, easy and satisfies your urge to garden.

There's a prayer, called the Serenity Prayer, that sums up the attitude we should assume as we grow older. One of the many variations goes like this: "God, grant me the serenity to accept the things I cannot change, Courage to change the things I can, And wisdom to know the difference." This could also be the prayer for the senior gardener when the inevitable frustration clouds our positive attitude.

THE PROGRESSION OF AGING & ITS EFFECTS ON YOUR GARDENING

*A*ge sneaks up on different gardeners in different ways. Joint problems seem to be the leading limiting factor. I lead off with that as the result of research rather than because it's what slowed me down. Other infirmities include cardiopulmonary conditions, skin problems, insect allergies and increased sensitivity to heat and cold.

For most, aging doesn't hit all at once. Rather, it progresses. As a child, I was really into toy cars and trucks, so I spent a lot of time on my knees playing with them. As a Boy Scout, I hiked a lot. In college, I walked many miles a day. Kneeling continued as an adult gardener. Problems began appearing about 15 years ago when it became difficult to stand up from a kneeling position. I kept a five-gallon bucket with me, regardless of whether or not I was weeding, and leaned on it to help me get up. As the knees got worse, however, it became harder and harder to kneel AND get back up. Now, I don't even try.

I've tried many of the tools and gadgets on the market, including a seat for gardening but had difficulty getting up from it. I have long handled tools but my legs begin hurting before I'm done.

As I began using my cane more often, my significant other convinced me to hire someone to mow the lawn and weed the planting beds. But, I continued to blow snow, reluctant to hire a plow contractor because I didn't want snow piled against my prized ginkgo tree near the driveway. My mowing contractor proved to be better than your average mow & blow guy, so I also contracted with him to plow snow, as well as mow and weed.*

If you have skin problems, they are most likely due to sun exposure through the years. Follow the advice of dermatologists now and slather with sunscreen, wear a broad brimmed hat, long sleeve shirt, long pants and sunglasses. Yes, sunglasses. UV rays also are bad for age related macular degeneration.

If you're sensitive to heat, schedule your gardening for early morning or just before dusk. If it's cold that bothers you, garden in the heat of the day, taking precautions, of course, to protect your skin and eyes, and stay hydrated,

My best advice for any gardening-limiting condition is to talk with your health care provider(s). They can best advise you on how far you can go, any limitations you should observe and precautions you should take. I found a good document with precautions online. The Ohio State University Extension document is entitled *Gardening with a Physical Limitation*. It has a lot of information on assistive technology, modified tasks and even a section on simple gardening style changes.

* He has since given up plowing due to the wear and tear on his truck and the high cost of insurance. But I found another good one.

ADAPTIVE GARDENING

*Y*ou know that we senior gardeners make up a significant share of the market when we're given a name. That name is the inspiration for the subtitle of this book – Adaptive Gardening.

Adaptive Gardening means just what you'd expect – adapting to the physical and mental challenges that are making it harder to do the gardening that you've enjoyed all your life. Each chapter recommends ways in which you can continue to enjoy gardening by modifying the way you garden and the garden itself.

Manufacturers are responding to the needs of seniors by making tools just for us. These include expandable tools that allow you to use them from a wheelchair, stool or garden cart. Other adaptable tools are lighter weight than standard tools and have foam grips. Still others are gear driven. I  have a pair of gear driven hedge clippers and they are so lightweight and easy to use that they've replaced the electric clippers.

 But how do you make sure that all of these special tools make it back to the shed or garage? After all, most of us are getting a little forgetful. My preferred method is to put all the tools I'll need for a job into a five-gallon bucket. For this to work, however, you have to replace the tool you're using when you reach for a new one. This bucket can also double as a stool to sit on while working or a prop if you need some help getting up from a kneeling position.

For those who don't want to carry a bucket of tools around with them, try painting the handles a bright color or tie brightly colored ribbons around the handles. This way, you can easily see them in the garden and the colors will jog your memory when it's time to gather up the tools and head in.

When transitioning into adaptive gardening, I recommend simplifying your garden. To keep from getting disoriented in your newly designed, simplified garden, retain some of your favorite plants and distinctive landmarks or focal points, all of which can orient you in the garden as your memory continues to diminish.

All of the ideas are presented as food for thought. I don't expect you to go out and do everything all at once. Rather, I want you to be aware of what's available when the need arises or when you realize that you'll soon have to make changes. I guess that's why the term adaptive gardening was coined rather than calling it revolutionary gardening.

MAKE THE MOST OF AGING-IN-PLACE'S OUTDOOR INITIATIVE

*A*ging-in-Place is a movement involving a number of organizations. It's aimed at helping seniors live in their own homes and communities for as long as possible. I think you'll agree that this is a much better choice than assisted living.

The movement began with architects and interior designers creating home modifications to help baby boomers stay in their homes as they age. The National Association of Home Builders (NAHB) has even gone so far as to develop a course of study for contractors, which leads to an examination. Contractors who pass the exam can then use the CAPS initials behind their names. CAPS stands for Certified-Aging-in-Place Specialist. According to a trade magazine, this certification program is now expanding to include outdoor spaces for landscapers.

This training includes many of the topics covered in this book. The training teaches landscape contractors about the need for such features as lighting, smooth paths, raised beds, shaded rest areas, low maintenance, and how to design them into a new or retrofit landscape plan. You can make the most of this initiative by hiring landscapers who have earned the CAPS designation.

If there are no CAPSs in your area yet, suggest taking the course and the exam to your favorite landscape professional. In the meantime, discuss your special needs and how they can best be incorporated into your landscape.

Aging-in-Place has taken giant leaps from just visiting nurses and meals-on-wheels. Today, your home and your yard can be modified to make it easier for you to live independently and with dignity. Adding your yard to the mix is the latest initiative in this program. In fact, it is so new that the landscape industry is just learning about it. You can help spread the news in your community and be rewarded with a senior-friendly yard and garden that will be the envy of the neighborhood.

KEEPING A JOURNAL NOW
CAN HELP IN THE FUTURE

*D*o you keep a journal? Many avid gardeners consider their journal to be nearly as important a tool as their trowel. I'm not advocating garden journaling as a practice to compensate for the forgetfulness of aging. Rather, I'm suggesting it for gardeners of all ages.

With that being said, it's a fact that our memories aren't as sharp as they were in our younger years, especially when trying to recall the exact dates of events that occurred a year ago. That's what the journal is for. It's to record when you performed important gardening tasks through the years. When you keep a journal in which you record the same information year after year, you'll see trends emerge.

You'll see the impact climate change has made and continues to make in your gardening schedule. You may be planting and harvesting earlier than you did when you first started the journal. You may be seeing migratory birds arriving earlier and maybe even species that you've never seen before. Biologists are telling us that southeastern flora and fauna are moving north and west.

Getting back to the subject of aging, a journal could be quite helpful when working with helpers. It can help them schedule with you the days they can come and the jobs they, and you, have to do. A journal can also be a handy aid to know what supplies you'll need for those assisted sessions.

Today, some gardeners continue to keep their journals in paper notebooks but an increasing number are turning to electronic journals. There are a number of garden journal templates online, some of which are free. Some are downloadable and printable. If you don't currently keep a journal, you might look at these. They contain all the pages you'll need with instructions for using them.

I'll share a number of ideas for making geriatric gardening easier physically. Journaling makes gardening easier mentally. It will also reduce the frustration that can come when you know that something should be done now but just can't think of what it is.

EXERCISE BEFORE & AFTER GARDENING

*I*sn't gardening exercise enough? No, say the experts – experts in both gardening and physical fitness. Have you noticed athletes in the Olympics and various other televised sports going through an exercise routine before taking to the field, ice or court? They must be on to something.

Gardeners use muscles in pursuit of their hobby that they may not use in any other activity. That's why it's good to stretch those muscles and limber them up with light exercise before starting the real exertion. It's the same reason why athletes warm up before their performances.

What about the senior gardener? Shouldn't you be saving your strength and conserving energy for the tasks ahead? No. Senior gardeners may be, arguably, more in need of warm up exercises than younger gardeners because seniors tend to be more sedentary between gardening sessions than younger gardeners.

Some of the exercises need to stretch shoulder, arm, neck and leg muscles. Others should get arthritic fingers moving as well as they can. Still others should help your breathing, especially if your aging limitations are caused by cardio/pulmonary, rather than or in addition to mobility problems.

Some gardening books that advocate exercise before and after gardening sessions also have suggested exercises in them. These may be fine for younger gardeners but I strongly recommend that senior gardeners visit a physical therapist for a recommended exercise regimen specifically for you.

If mobility is challenging, visit your orthopedist. If breathing is your problem, visit your cardiologist or pulmonologist. These doctors will write a requisition explaining your exact needs to the physical therapist. Be sure and tell the doctor that you would like a pre and post gardening exercise regimen.

Many Medicare supplement plans pay for a specific number of PT sessions or a certain number of weeks. You may need to pay a copay but it's worth it to be sure the exercises are specific to your needs and physical condition. This is much better than doing generic exercises that could do more harm than good. The therapist may also give you daily exercises that will help you feel better, even on days when you're not gardening.

SAFE LIFTING

*I*t's tough to keep a gardener from lifting stuff, even a senior gardener who shouldn't be lifting anything heavier than a water bottle. Just because we were born into the stubborn generation doesn't mean we can't lift safely, if we must.

Here are some tips for safe lifting gleaned from sources directed toward a wide range of lifters, from senior gardeners to warehouse workers.

- Know your limits. Don't try to lift anything that feels as though it's going to be too heavy.
- Balance and falling should always be in the forefront of your mind. Avoid trying to lift any awkward items.
- Remember the old adage, lift with your knees, not your back. Most mobility problems have their start with the back. Bend your knees into a squat position and keep your back straight. Standing close to the object, grab hold and slowly stand up.
- If you feel yourself tipping too far in any direction, let go of the object you're lifting and stand straight up, slowly. The object you're lifting can be replaced. Your back can't. If there's something nearby to steady yourself, grab it.
- Don't walk with the object you just lifted. Place it in a wheelbar row or garden cart to transport it to its destination.
- Avoid twisting when lifting. This can mess up our back permanently. My son sustained such an injury when he was in his 20s

and, despite surgery, it still bothers him almost three decades later.

- Avoid reaching and looking up for things. This can cause back strain and cause you to fall backward.
- Avoid lifting from the floor into a full upright position. Lift from the floor to a platform like a garden cart. Take a little rest and finish the lift.
- Don't lift for a long period of time and take frequent rest/water breaks.

My personal preference for getting tools to the garden and such things as weeds out of the garden is a 5 gallon bucket (Pictured above). It's lightweight, and it isn't large enough to carry a heavy load. So, I'm was never tempted to over do it. The tools in the picture are the tools I carry in it. When I could still kneel, I had the choice of using the bucket to help me get up from a kneeling position or simply turning it over and using it as a stool. Best of all it was free. If you don't have access to an empty 5 gallon bucket, you can buy one at a big box home store for under $5.

The best tip of all is to avoid lifting if at all possible. Hopefully you've established a relationship with a hired gardener or have family members you can call on to help you keep active in your lifelong pursuit of gardening. Leave major lifting to your helpers.

HOW TO ADAPT

SIMPLIFY YOUR GARDEN FOR LESS MAINTENANCE

*I*n the Bible, Jesus tells the Pharisees that the Sabbath was made for people, not people for the Sabbath. The same can be said of gardens. When we're young and just starting to garden, the time it takes to maintain a complex garden doesn't matter. We have all kinds of energy and, for many, weeding, mowing, pruning and other garden tasks are good respites from our fast paced world. As we turn the corner onto the downward slope leading to old age, those tasks look ever more daunting.

What's a gardener to do? Simple: simplify. Determine the elements in your garden that you're really attached to. Either design your senior garden around these elements or move them to a different location in your new garden.

Depending on the extent of your garden renovations, this might be a good time to retain a landscape designer to help you design the most efficient new gardens and a landscape contractor to do the heavy work. If you have in your community designers and contractors who hold the CAPS (Certified Aging-in-Place Specialists) designation, they may be able to share with you ideas that you never thought of.

If you're going to undertake this process alone, there are a number of factors to consider. Many perennials grow and spread fast, so they have to be dug up and split frequently. This can be a difficult chore as you grow older. Many aging gardeners take care of the problem by getting rid of the perennials. Dig them up one last time, split them and give all four segments away.

If kneeling to plant annuals is a chore, plant them in containers and then put the containers out in the bed. Be sure to use lightweight plastic or fiberglass containers, rather than ceramic or terra cotta. I've been using the pot-in-pot technique. This way, I can position the decorative container and then just slip the nursery pot into it.

Planting annuals in containers also makes deadheading easier. You can do that by sitting on a stool or just leaning over. You don't have to kneel. Plus, the flowers are concentrated so you don't have to crawl around the bed.

Grass is very labor intensive. It has to be mowed every week during the growing season. It has to be weeded almost as frequently. The answer? Reduce the size of your lawn by building new beds using low maintenance shrubs and ground cover. Ground cover is very low maintenance. Apply mulch when you plant the ground cover and the two will work together to discourage weeds,

The woody shrubs that you plant will require pruning. This should be done with sharp, bypass pruning shears. Bypass shears are those that cut like scissors. Use loppers for the larger branches and stalks.

Be sure you prune using modern techniques. When removing a branch from a main stem, cut outside the branch collar. The branch collar is the swelling where the branch grows out of a larger stem. The collar contains chemicals that help the wound heal by callousing. If you are removing a vertical stem, remove it at the base or where it attaches to a larger stem. Don't leave stubs. Stubs are perfect openings for insects and diseases.

Dress properly when pruning. Wear eye protection and gloves, as well as long sleeves and pants. This will reduce injuries from the sharp ends of shoots and branches.

Shrub pruning is one job that you might want to leave to the professionals. Tree pruning is a job that you definitely want to leave to professional arborists, especially if you have to climb a ladder. When I read of a property owner being injured or killed while pruning trees in their yard, the majority are senior citizens. Even if you are pruning from the ground, a branch can fall and hit you on the head or in the face. Tree work is definitely not a do-it-yourself job. It should be left only to trained, professional arborists.

MAINTAIN YOUR GARDEN
AS MOTHER NATURE WOULD

*M*aintaining your landscape as Mother Nature would may seem counterintuitive. We think of Mother Nature as doing everything perfectly. However, Mother Nature's idea of perfect is different from ours. People don't need to maintain woodlands, desert or other natural environments, aside from picking up trash left by humans? The flora and fauna in these ecosystems take care of themselves and each other.

Adopt the ideas and philosophy that I'll present here and you'll have a natural landscape that has minimal maintenance needs. First, add a new word to your vocabulary: Imperfect. When did you see a natural environment that was perfectly groomed? Natural plants aren't shaped like lollipops or sheared into closely cropped hedges. Rather, natural environments tend to be imperfect by our standards.

Design As Mother Nature Does
To the untrained eye, natural landscapes may appear to be haphazard. That is indeed the case. When you see a forest with trees in perfect rows, they were planted by humans. Seeds germinate where they drop or are blown by the wind or carried by birds. That's why forest trees don't grow in straight rows. You can have a more natural look in your landscape as well.

Don't Mow Too Short
Lawn care professionals recommend that lawns be mowed three inches high. This results in thicker lawns that discourage weeds.

Although some people prefer the putting green look, longer grass is actually easier to maintain, as well as healthier. The guy with the short crew cut has to go to the barber more often than one with longer hair. Formally groomed shrubs and other plants also have to be trimmed more often or they look shaggy. Those that have never been groomed or shaped always look natural.

Reduce the Size of Your Lawn
Less grass can reduce your maintenance needs even more. Lawns require fertilizer, insect and disease control, weekly mowing and, in some places, frequent watering. Reduce the amount of your property that is devoted to turf and you'll reduce the amount of maintenance you have to do. Replace the lawn you remove with shrubs that need minimal maintenance.

Use Native Plants
Sticking with native plants is one of the easiest ways to maintain a natural environment. Now, I'm not one of those people who believes that the only good plant is a native plant. The most prized tree in my yard is a ginkgo, whose ancestors came from prehistoric Asia. Some introduced plants have naturalized well and behave themselves in our landscapes. Unless you are willing to research which introduced plants have naturalized well and behave themselves, you may want to simplify your garden by sticking with natives. Natives need less water, less fertilizer and less insect and disease control. And, if you plant them close enough together, they'll discourage weeds.

What Are Weeds, Anyway?
One way to maintain your garden like Mother Nature is to apply this definition to your dislike for weeds: A weed is a plant growing where you don't want it. The photo on the previous page shows one of my landscape beds. Last weekend, my gardener weeded it but it sometimes gets a bit weedy between visits. To cover my behind, the sign in front of the trees reads, "Experimental dandelion farm. Don't disturb weeds."

Get Professional Design Help
It makes sense to sit down with a good, professional landscape designer when you're ready to simplify your landscape for easy maintenance. Explain your goals, share your ideas and then turn the designer loose.

EMBRACE IMPERFECTION

*I*t may be asking a lot but, after a gardening life of striving for the most perfect garden possible, I'm now suggesting that you chuck all that and embrace imperfection. Why? Because perfection, the way we humans like to garden, is tedious, tiring and time consuming. Imperfection, Mother Nature's way, is simple. As you age, the tedium of perfection takes a toll on your body and increases the stress your aging body doesn't need.

In her book, *Gardening for a Lifetime*, the late Sydney Eddison wrote, "Of all the lessons that gardening has taught me, the hardest to digest inwardly has been the acceptance of imperfection." She went on to write, "I'm gradually learning to go with the flow and to appreciate the glorious moments for what they are, brief and beautiful." When you accept, as Sydney did, the imperfection of nature, you'll enjoy gardening for your lifetime with minimal fretting and fussing.

When Sydney Eddison accepted nature's imperfection, she began blowing leaves back under shrubs rather than having to blow them into piles, which she would then have to pick up and carry to the compost pile, only to have to carry them back to the plants after decomposition.

Another example (pictured on the next page) is in my backyard. I have a rather steep hill. When I had the landscape installed in 2002, I had the hill landscaped all the way up to the plateau at the top. Included was a row of junipers about midway up. The plan was to keep the whole hill weeded and neatly trimmed. However, as the plants grew bigger, and my ability to safely climb the hill became more difficult, I decided to let the upper half (above the junipers) revert to wild and have my gardener keep the bottom half weeded. This has worked out well, and is a good example of embracing imperfection and adaptive gardening.

Mother Nature doesn't plant in rows, so why should we? We love to take walks in the woods. Then, why do we come home to our own gardens and seek precision? Embrace imperfection and you'll be gardening nature's way.

The "perfect" hill shortly after planting.

The imperfect hill today.

DOWNSIZED SENIOR GARDENS CAN BE BEAUTIFUL

*I*f you are thinking about downsizing, banish from your thoughts that your gardening career is finished. If you're moving to a smaller house on a smaller lot, you can do wonders with those spaces. In fact, small space gardens are all the rage these days. And, it's not just seniors who are opting for smaller gardens; younger people are also.

The younger gardeners are embracing smaller gardens because of time constraints. Smaller gardens require less maintenance, and that should be a goal for all senior gardeners as well.

I've seen many small, urban gardens all over the country. Some have even illustrated *The Geriatric Gardener*. Two senior gardeners in Rochester, New York's 19th ward have very nice, easy-to-maintain, small space gardens.

These two gardeners, who live only a couple of blocks apart, have very different approaches to gardening, as you can see from the photos on the previous page. Marian Boutet's garden (left column of photos) is very informal and she is just starting to renovate to incorporate adaptive measures, including wider, smoother pathways. Marcy Klein (right column of photos), who has 10 gardens and nearly 200 plant varieties in her compact space, is already well along with adapting to her changing needs.

If you need more convincing that small space gardens can be beautiful, invest in a copy of the book, *Buffalo Style Gardens*. Written by Sally Cunningham and Jim Charlier, it is like a mini-tour in words and pictures of Buffalo's amazing Garden Walk, where visitors have an opportunity to visit hundreds of private gardens each summer. Many are small, urban gardens. Sally and Jim are both current or past officers of the Garden Walk organization.

Even if you're considering a townhouse or apartment, you can still garden. Most townhouses have a deck or patio that you can decorate with containerized plants. Many apartments have balconies or terraces on which you can plant a containerized garden. These options also are popular with young adults who don't have the time to tend a larger garden.

Don't forget house plants. Your indoor garden also needs some TLC. The only reason to give up gardening is by choice, never by circumstances.

TOOLS FOR SENIOR GARDENERS

*Y*ou probably have gardening tools that are your old favorites. Lately, they may feel as though they've become too heavy, too bulky or you just can't handle them correctly. The tools haven't changed. You have. This means it's time to invest in new tools.

When it was comfortable to kneel, many of us preferred short handle tools that brought us right down close to the soil. These tools also gave us more leverage. When kneeling becomes painful or impossible, however, we need to switch to long handle tools.

An ergonomic trowel helps relieve pain from wrist twisting.

When selecting long handle tools, check the fit right there in the store to save an extra trip to return them if they turn out to be uncomfortable. Be sure you can stand straight when using the tools. Having to bend over can be very painful to your back. And, be sure the tools aren't too heavy.

Select ergonomically designed tools with fiberglass handles. Check those with and without foam sleeves and pick the one that's most comfortable for you. If you have arthritis in your fingers and hands, the foam covered handles should be easier to grip.

You can also buy garden tools with plastic handle extenders if you work from a wheeled garden seat. These will allow you to remain on a path and reach in to the plants. These tools are good for working in

A short and long handle CobraHead single blade cultivator is easy to use. I prefer the short handle but my knees and back don't. The long handle, while very good, is made only with a heavy, wooden handle

raised beds, too. Special gardening tools are also available for gardeners who use a wheelchair.

For maintenance tools like pruners, hedge trimmers and loppers, look at ratchet or geared models. These increase the pressure you exert two or three times, making pruning and trimming jobs almost effortless.

Consider a two-wheeled wheelbarrow made of plastic or lightweight aluminum to replace your single wheel steel model. A lightweight cart with four large wheels may be even better than a wheelbarrow.

If you grow plants from seed in your garden, check out the many seeders on the market. They range from trowels that dispense seeds to both long and short syringe types to wheeled units for the home garden.

Geared or ratcheted hand tools are very comfortable.

Hooking up a hose to water your garden can be a near impossible task for senior gardeners. So many houses today have the spigot only inches from the ground. Getting down low enough to make the connection and holding on to the connector with arthritic fingers present challenges. That's the way it is for me, and I suspect for you, too.

Dramm, a manufacturer of gardening watering systems, has developed a hose protector/extender. It has a strong but malleable aluminum coil that can be threaded onto the spigot and left there to make life easier! Once you have the extender (sometimes called a "hose protector"), a quick connect/disconnect system. threads into your hose end and the other into your hose protector/extender. Then all you do to connect the hose is to snap them together. You can probably do that without even kneeling, although you may be more comfortable sitting on a stool.

WATERING WITH SOAKER HOSES

*L*iving in New York's Finger Lakes region, I tend to forget that most areas of the country have to water their landscapes on a regular basis. Mother Nature takes pity on us geezers in my area most of the time. For those times that she forgets us, I have a network of soaker hoses.

Soaker hoses may be considered the poor person's irrigation system. That's not meant as an affront to those of you who live in hot, dry climates where irrigation systems are essential. It's meant to convey that soaker hoses are modestly priced so everyone can afford them.

These hoses aren't very attractive. They're black, rough textured rubber, reflecting their previous life as vehicle tires. That's right, soaker hoses are made from recycled tires. But then, they are intended to be buried under mulch.

To get started, lay out the hoses so they run near the root zone of the plants you want watered. If you have enough hose, it's OK to wrap them loosely around the plants, keeping them in the root zone, not up against the trunk or stem. Use lengths of regular garden hose to cross driveways, walkways, patios and any other places you don't want wet.

Connect the hose to an outdoor water spigot and turn it on only about a quarter turn. Turn it on any more and you'll blow holes in the soaker hoses. The water just oozes out through the porous, recycled rubber. It operates much like an irrigation system's drip emitter.

Needless to say, you have to leave the water on for a long time for the plants to receive the recommended inch a week. But you waste less water this way than using sprinklers. Much of the water sprayed into the air from a sprinkler evaporates before it reaches the ground. Besides, who wants to hold a hose or reposition the sprinkler every little while.

Soaker hoses are great for planting beds, trees and shrubs but aren't very practical for lawns. Use sprinklers if you really need to water your lawn. As you get older, you'll probably want to reduce the size of your lawn anyway. A few sky high water bills may be just the impetus you need.

You should know best the watering needs of landscapes where you live. In our area, I recommend prioritizing. Trees are the most valuable plants, so put them at the top of your list. Large, mature trees probably don't need irrigation. Their roots are sufficiently deep to find water. It's the young and newly planted trees that may need irrigation help. Shrubs should be second on your list, followed by perennials.

I'm committed to simpler gardening so I swear by soaker hoses when I have to water. They are also good when you are under municipal water restrictions.

SOME THOUGHTS ON "TO DO" LISTS

*T*o Do lists, sometimes called Honey Do lists, are a fact of life in our busy society. There are so many distractions today that it's very easy to forget the things you wanted to do today. However, the goal of adaptive gardening is to shrink that list as we shrink in size. That's how we simplify our gardening and adapt to our diminishing abilities.

We senior gardeners need a To Do list just like anybody else. The big difference between us and those younger than us is that we have to budget our time better. While younger gardeners can put everything on the list and then whittle away, it would be best if we seniors listed all of the garden tasks that need to get done on a wish list and then prioritize, scheduling only what we know we can get done in that time period. We should also note which tasks we can do and which we should enlist help to get done.

We can then call our helper(s) and schedule them. For the tasks we plan to handle ourselves, we can schedule a few and put them on a "Do" list. List them in blocks of a half hour to an hour, depending on your stamina and your ability to get them done within the allotted time. Schedule your rest and hydration breaks on the To Do list, too.

This may seem like a bit more pencil pushing than you want to do but, believe me, doing it will be well worth the time and effort. Simplifying your gardening tasks should be your major concern. That means not ending the day exhausted or in pain.

Working in short, comfortable blocks of time with plenty of time to rest, cool off and rehydrate should be one of your top goals. This regimen is healthy for your joints and muscles, your heart and lungs, your kidneys and the list goes on. If none of these are bothering you at this time, that's the best time to begin the work/rest routine. You may be able to stave off the aforementioned problems for awhile.

If you already have mobility, movement, cardio-pulmonary or other problems, don't just sluff it off and say, "Oh, well, I have (name problem) already so what's the difference whether I push myself or not?" Adopt the work/rest routine now and you'll be surprised how much better you'll feel. If you adopt this routine, adapt it to your needs and stick with it, I predict that you'll begin feeling better after a day in the garden. Not 21 again but better than you did when you were pushing yourself.

Few senior gardeners will dispute the importance of a To Do list to keep on track. Perhaps it would be easier to adapt to our changing needs if we renamed it our Need Doing or Should Get Done list. Then we wouldn't be tied to it so rigidly. At the end of the day, we can cross off what we've done and save the rest for another day.

HARDSCAPES FOR YOUR SENIOR GARDEN

*H*ardscapes are anything in your garden that isn't alive, and there are some hardscape accommodations to consider when you are designing your senior garden. If you engage a professional designer, be sure they are aware of these needs. If they are certified aging-in-place specialists, they should know these things. If not, you may have to remind them.

Here are some of the hardscape considerations you'll need in the future, even if you don't need them now:

- Make paths wide, smooth and flat. As walking gets more difficult, you should avoid uneven surfaces. If breathing becomes a problem, you don't want to be walking up and down significant grades. A walker or wheelchair may be in your future. Wider paths, as well as smooth, flat surfaces are needed to accommodate them. Be sure there is an alternative to steps.

- Be sure there's a comfortable, shaded rest area. As your stamina wanes, you'll have to take frequent rest breaks. Be sure this area is easy to get to from anywhere in the garden.

- Lighting needs to be brighter. Your senior landscape should be better lit than your previous landscape. Specific needs will be detailed in the next chapter

Taking accommodation into consideration before modifying your garden can save you a lot of time and money. It may also save your life and extend your gardening career.

THE IMPORTANCE OF LIGHTING YOUR GARDEN

*H*ave you noticed that the sun is getting dimmer? Even in this day of global warming? Well, maybe it's your eyes. Even if you aren't experiencing the need for stronger lighting now, you will in the future. One way to ensure your safety in your garden, especially if you like to enjoy your garden in the evening, is to install garden lighting.

Outdoor lighting choices are endless today. They range from small accent lights for your deck or patio to motion detector activated spotlights for security. You are going to have to check out your landscape at night to see what combination of lights best suits your needs.

The most basic lighting is the stake light for illuminating paths, trails, patio edges, and stairs. Avoid the inexpensive sets of solar lights in drug and variety stores. I've found that these need plenty of sun in order to keep the batteries charged and they need to be replaced every season. Low power lights are more reliable. These have to be plugged in. Weather-proof timers can turn them on and off and the wires are buried and out of site.

If you do a lot of evening reading outdoors, you'll need stronger light than the low power emits. Be sure these lights are hard wired or that you unplug them when they aren't in use. Be sure your outdoor receptacles are equipped with Ground Fault Circuit Interrupters (GFCI). They can save your life, and they are required by building code in most jurisdictions. Personally, I would call in a professional electrician to install lighting and receptacles.

I admit I'm not a lighting expert. However, I am writing this to start your creative juices. I do know that I need more light than I did a few years ago, and so will you. And, as I mentioned above, I'd hire an electrician to do any electrical work. You should, too.

RAISED BEDS LET YOU SIT DOWN ON THE JOB

As your knees start to wear out, you may try a number of tactics to reduce the pain as you garden. They include knee pads, raised kneelers and portable seats. But have you tried raised beds yet?

Raised planting bed designs and materials can run the gamut. Wood rectangles are the most common. These usually are very utilitarian, but you can make fancy, attractive wood boxes for raised beds. Decorative landscape stone like those used for retaining walls also make very attractive raised planting beds.

The cap – the top layer of wood or stone – is a very important feature. It should be wide enough for you to sit on and garden. The width of the raised bed itself is another important consideration. If it's free-standing, the width can be half your reach so you can sit on the cap and reach to the middle to garden and/or harvest. If the bed is against a structure, you'll have to be able to reach all the way across.

The photo of decorative wood, raised beds at the Paul J. Ciener Botanical Garden in Kernersville, North Carolina, illustrate the different widths between the free-standing beds on the left and those against the wall on the right.

Vertical gardens are quite popular today for those who are able to stand and garden. Vertical gardens can be as simple as a trellis or as sophisticated as a completely planted wall. The pictured vertical garden (below) is at the Coastal Maine Botanical Garden in Booth Bay, Maine.

Raised planting beds offer another advantage. If your native soil isn't to your plants' liking, you don't have to mess around with compost and other amendments. Just buy the soil that is most compatible with the plants you plan to grow. This will reduce your maintenance considerably, while also saving additional wear and tear on your aging body. You won't have to mix in amendments; you can garden sitting down; plants will grow thick, strong and happy so you'll probably have fewer weeds and maybe even fewer insects. What could be better than that?

MEMORY AIDS FOR YOUR GARDEN

*T*he aging process may affect us mentally as well as physically. It may not rise to the level of Alzheimer or even dementia. It may just be forgetfulness. Like forgetting our tools when we go from one gardening task to another.

You can keep track of tools by carrying them in a carpenter's apron. You can also use a hand carried tool holder. These appendages should serve as a reminder to take your tools when you go in the house or move on to your next chore. Just remember to check to be sure all of your tools are there.

These carriers work fine for small tools but what about long handled tools like shovels and rakes? Lightweight tools with fiberglass handles often have bright colored handles to help you keep track of them. Most are yellow but I've also seen other bright colors. If you're still using your tried and true wood handled tools, Paint the handles a bright color or tie brightly colored ribbon around them. Although ribbons can be applied faster than paint, they aren't as permanent as paint.

Have you ever gotten lost in your garden or on your way there from your house or shed? Jack Kerrigan, a former region director with the Ohio State University Extension Service, suggested to HGTV writer Jeff Stafford that "a distinctive and familiar focal point allows for easier orientation." Kerrigan also said that plants that trigger memories such as a favorite herb or vegetable are always beneficial to keep you oriented.

When simplifying your landscape, leaving some favorite plants in place to serve as focal points may be important to you in the future, even if they aren't of concern to you now. A conifer with a distinctive conical shape or that distinctive evergreen smell may keep you oriented. The fragrance of herbs planted near your back door may become an important beacon when you least expect it. You also might consider using a familiar piece of garden sculpture as a " beacon" (see photo on next page).

Disorientation isn't something that usually gives you warning. More often than not it just comes upon you, and it's very scary. Especially if you find yourself lost in your own backyard. That's why having these aids in place before you need them is so important.

ADAPTATIONS FOR THE VISUALLY IMPAIRED

*L*imbs and tickers aren't the only parts of our bodies that are affected by advancing years. Eyesight is also on the decline for many. Like everything else, this doesn't have to preclude your continuing to garden. It just means you have to adapt.

You've noticed that the lights are beginning to dim in the house but the electricity's just fine. So, it must be your eyes. It's a good idea to begin planning how you'll adapt your garden for visual impairment now, while you can still see relatively well.

Garden paths should be adapted for walkers and wheelchairs. Adapting them for visual impairment at the same time can save you money over having to make additional adaptations when the need arises. Here are some suggestions::

- Use a different paving material for each path. For example, smooth concrete on one path, rough concrete on another and pavers on another.

- Make the whole patio stamped concrete with each path a unique pattern.

- Avoid making paths curvy. Curves can interfere with orientation.

- Put a handrail on one side of each path to use as a guide.

A distinctive plant at each intersection or in each planting bed can help your orientation. They might be unique to the touch. Each could have its own fragrance. This will help you identify intersections and know where to turn to return to your house.

Each bed could also be identified by a unique sound. One could have a wind chime. Another could have a water feature with the sound of running water. And, a third could have an artistic bell like the Soleri Windbell in the photo (Next page). It would be a good idea to place wind operated devices right at an intersection so you could feel them if there is no wind to give you auditory guidance.

In addition to saving money by installing vision aids when installing mobility aids, planning ahead has another advantage. You'll have time to get used to these features before you need them. Each time you take a particular path through your garden, make a mental note of the unique feel, smell or other adaptive features. Soon you'll be guided by the stimuli.

If you have a vegetable garden, there are other adaptations that will make gardening easier and more enjoyable for the person with failing eyesight. They include:

- Plant vegetables in straight rows. The new practice among younger gardeners is to do just the opposite and plant them like you would a flower garden, even intermingling the veggies with the flowers. However, straight rows help guide the person with poor vision.

- Use a notched board to space out seedlings. This isn't something new. I've seen it used on TV gardening programs for years.

- Another age old technique is to run a string between two stakes at each end of the row as a guide for planting seeds. My father did that when I was a kid. But it's even more important for gardeners with failing eyesight. The string acts as a guide.

- Identify each row with a raised-letter plant tag.

The Oregon State University Extension Service has an excellent bulletin (EM 8498), entitled *Adaptive Gardening for the visually impaired*, that is very complete.

BALANCE PROBLEMS WHEN GARDENING?
CHECK THIS OUT

*L*est you haven't experienced it yet, balance is one of the most common problems faced by seniors. That may be why falls are among the most frequent injuries to seniors. And, the more active we are the more apt we are to suffer balance problems than the more sedentary person.

The Geriatric Gardener ready to head out to the garden.

Most senior balance problems can be traced to a number of diseases, such as vertigo. But some senior gardeners report lack of balance only when they work in the garden. Some of these people will be diagnosed with an age-related disease while others will not be diagnosed with any evidence of a disease. Their diagnosis may be dehydration.

Falls and dehydration are nothing to be taken lightly. The first thing to do when you feel symptoms is to get to your health care provider. Rule out the diseases that cause dizziness and confirm that dehydration is the cause. Dehydration is an easy problem to treat. The prescription will surely be to drink more water. If your electrolytes are out of whack due to dehydration, your health care provider may suggest a sports drink that has electrolytes in it.

Whenever you work in the garden, make sure you have plenty of water, as well as shady places in the garden where you can sit, rest and rehydrate. If it's hot enough to dehydrate you, it's also hot enough for you to need sunglasses, sunscreen and a wide brimmed hat. And, know when to pack it in for the day. We seniors are also prone to heat exhaustion on hot days.

There's also evidence that diet and exercise can contribute to your balance, so be sure you eat healthy and exercise regularly. You are also encouraged to do warm up exercises before you begin your gardening session to help prevent falls.

Just to be on the safe side, remember to take your cell phone and/or medical alert with you whenever you work in the garden.

Gardening is meant to be an enjoyable pastime, not a job that has to get done at all costs. So please put your health before that of your garden. Plants are hardier than we often give them credit for, while we are less hardy as we grow older. Putting things in perspective will result in a healthier garden and a healthier, upright you.

CONSIDER GETTING A FALL ALERT

*H*ow steady are you on your feet? Or even getting up from a kneeling position? If you've ever fallen and not been able to get up by yourself, it may be a good idea to look into a fall alert. Remember the "I've fallen and I can't get up" commercials? Well, today you have a number of choices.

Several brands are advertised on television and in the newspaper. Others are on Facebook. You can also Google "fall alert" for manufacturers' websites. You'll find interesting reviews and stories on how to choose an alert by Consumer Reports and AARP.

When my family pushed me to get one, I did my due diligence and was particularly pleased with Consumer Reports. They compared all the major brands so you could see apples-to-apples comparisons. This was very helpful in making my choice.

The system I chose has no set up fee and no contract. Just a monthly fee paid automatically from my credit card account. Each company offers several levels of service. The basic service is tied to your home phone, so it only works in your house or yard. That's pretty much the range of a cordless phone.

I chose the second level of service. It's like a small cell phone with GPS. If I need help, I press the button and a friendly voice says, "Hi, Duane. How can I help you?" You can set up the protocol any way you want. Mine is set up so that, if I need help, they call my son who lives in the same town as me and is my business partner. If he doesn't answer, they'll call 911.

The third option is a unit that senses you falling and automatically alerts the call center. In the Consumer Reports post, a doctor stated that fall detectors may not work perfectly every time. He said this feature may register something as a fall that isn't.

The most common monitor styles are worn around the neck or around the wrist. I chose the neck version because I don't like anything around my wrists. Since I've had mine, I've seen commercials for another brand that also offers a unit the size of a pager that you clip on your belt or can be carried in your pocket. In the event of a fall, this unit may be difficult to grab if you are laying on that side.

This is one of those purchases that you hope you never have to use. But, it lends a sense of security when gardening. I've read of senior gardeners sustaining injuries and not being discovered until several hours later when a family member checks on them.

ALLERGIES CAN STRIKE AT ANY TIME.
GET CHECKED IF YOU HAVE SYMPTOMS

*H*ave you recently begun coughing, wheezing and/or sneezing during or after gardening? Does your nose run? Eyes water? Do you develop a rash after working outside? This could be caused by environmental allergies, even in your senior years.

You may have thought of allergies as affecting only children. That's not true. You can develop allergies at any age. I was 50. More and more adults seem to be getting allergies. I have no proof, only an observation.

Environmental allergies are caused by your immune system reacting to something in the environment like pollen, mold, dust mites and/or pet dander. If you start exhibiting symptoms, you don't have to suffer. And, it doesn't indicate that your gardening career is over. However, it is a serious enough problem that you should go to your primary care physician, who may send you to a specialist like an allergist.

Allergies may be treated with over-the-counter or prescription medication. Or, you may need the infamous allergy shots. These really aren't so bad. I've been getting them for 30 years. It all depends on what your doctor believes will work best. You may be asked to undergo a series of tests to try and pinpoint exactly what you are allergic to. Some medications, however, prevent doctors from doing these diagnostic tests.

The take away from this is that allergies are serious but not debilitating. It's important to seek medical attention and take the medications prescribed. If you do that, you should be able to continue enjoying gardening. If you don't, life can be miserable. Just mowing the lawn can make you exhibit symptoms.

There are some things you can do to help the medicine be even more effective. Don't push the limits. If the weather reports indicate that we can expect high pollen counts, stay indoors that day. Your garden will still be growing the following day. If it's hot and muggy, stay indoors then, too. Allergy therapy is medication tempered with a good dose of common sense. Just as you wouldn't go into a burning building, you shouldn't go into an allergy-infested environment.

Flowers like those pictured below are beautiful, but they aren't an allergy sufferer's friend. You definitely don't want to get your nose in there for a sniff.

GARDENING IN THE SUN

*R*emember when being out in the sun was a good thing? When you looked forward to starting your annual tan? It was a rite of summer. Now, is your dermatologist your BFF?

How things have changed. The sun used to be our friend. Well, it still is; it's nature's energy source. But, too much of a good thing can have the opposite effect. You know the old saying – everything in moderation.

Today, some people consider the sun their enemy, especially those who are now having to undergo dermatology procedures to remove skin the sun began damaging decades ago.

What's a sun-sensitive gardener to do? Cover up. Depending on how sensitive you are, you may be able to get away with a wide-brim hat and lots of sun screen. If you've been experiencing skin problems, you should consider wearing long pants and a long sleeve shirt when gardening. Today, you can buy these clothes in lightweight fabrics that let the breeze through but not the sun's harmful rays.

Don't forget sunglasses. Bright sunlight can exacerbate such conditions as macular degeneration. Also, the skin around your eyes is sensitive, so you don't want the Doc coming close with the liquid nitrogen.

Follow our previously published recommendations, including frequent rests in a shady spot. Limit your time in the sun even if you aren't having problems right now. Skin problems can begin at any age.

DON'T BE A MARTYR. RETREAT TO YOUR
AIR CONDITIONING WHEN IT'S TOO HOT.

*P*reviously, I've recommended frequent breaks from your gardening to rest and rehydrate in shady spots with seating and cool water for those breaks. That's all well and good under normal conditions. But, when the heat is brutal, there's only one thing to do. Pack it in and head for the air conditioning. You can always buy replacement plants but there's only one you. As much as you enjoy gardens and gardening, none is worth putting your health, and even your life, in danger.

Many of us are from a generation that was taught that we had to get the job done no matter what. That admonition didn't take into consideration the aging process, physical limitations or even global warming.

Summers are hotter than they were when we were younger. Despite sunscreen and proper clothing, sun can continue to damage our skin.

We need to drink more water when it's hot for the same reason that we have to water our plants more often. I'm one of the biggest delinquents on that front, and it really came crashing down on me this morning when I got a very painful cramp in my good leg. Everyone I've met so far today, including an EMT, diagnosed my lack of proper hydration. Now, water hydrates me and trips to the bathroom give me the exercise I need to work out the cramp. Let's face it; we're senior citizens! Teens may be invincible but not us, and it's about time that we figure that out.

By the way, I share my aversion to water with my exterior plants but have been accused of watering my houseplants too often. As summer continues, enjoy the moderate days in your garden. And when the sun sizzles, retreat to the air conditioning and give your houseplants some TLC that they'll appreciate. You and your gardens, both outdoors and indoors, will be healthier for it.

STAY HYDRATED

*A*s winter wanes and we get back out into our gardens, it's important to remember that the first thing on our ingredient label, as well as those on our plants, is water. Our plants and our bodies are more than half water. Water is also what we lose when the sun bakes us and our plants. Call it sweat or perspiration, it's the water you're losing. And it needs replacing.

When you were a kid, you may have been able to play outdoors all day without drinking

anything. But you ain't a kid no more. And you can't work outside all day without drinking anything.

Put a bottle of water in your tool carrier. It's just as important as your trowel and other tools. It's the tool that keeps you healthy. If you prefer, electrolyte replacement drinks like those poured on football coaches are OK. But avoid sugary soft drinks or alcohol. They don't quench your thirst. Save them as a treat when you're done gardening.

t's recommended that we seniors take frequent rest breaks in a shady spot while gardening. It's also recommended that we drink six to eight glasses of water a day. So why not put a cooler of nice, cold water in your rest area to refresh you as you relax?

Drinking water cools you from the inside out. If just drinking water isn't doing the trick, try cooling from the outside in, too. Look into phase change clothing. Phase change clothing has material inside that changes from solid to liquid as it absorbs the heat from your body. You put it in the freezer to change the liquid to a solid and then wear it as you garden and the phase change material will turn back to liquid as it keeps you cool.

Phase change apparel can be found on the internet or you can check garden centers that sell clothing, or outdoor supply stores. I suggest that you start small to be sure you like this material. Most of the companies are promoting vests in the $150 range on the internet. But many also have neck bands for under $20.

When it comes to healthy gardening, drinking water is right up there with slathering sunscreen, wearing shades and a wide brimmed hat, and taking frequent rest breaks.

PLANTING ANNUALS

Planting annuals is a spring tradition for many senior gardeners. Much of the fun is going to the garden center and browsing the fragrant aisles of annuals in six packs and nursery pots. I hope that tradition doesn't start to fade into only a memory this season. Kneeling on the ground to plant them may have sidelined you but it doesn't have to bench the tradition.

Why not recruit children and grandchildren to help you with the planting? When you are as certain as possible that the chance of frost or a freeze has passed, pick a day that the majority of family can help. Designate one family member to pick you up and plan to meet the rest at the garden center.

It will be the first day of a whole new tradition as you help each family member select their favorite flowers. When you get home, ask for one or more volunteers to prepare the planting beds by tilling or turning the soil and raking it smooth. Then have them mix in compost or fertilizer. If it's more convenient for the tilling volunteers, they can do this task before you go to buy the plants.

When it's time to plant, have everyone lay out their plant selections in the bed under your supervision. This will allow you to move them around if you want to make changes after seeing them in place. When satisfied, have family members take turns digging holes twice as big around as the roots but only as deep as the roots, placing the plant in the hole and backfilling. When everyone has planted all of your purchases, designate a couple of people to mulch and water. Since these plants are small, you will probably not need more than an inch or two of mulch.

You'll have to water your annuals if you have a dry summer. They should receive at least an inch of water a week. Someone can set up the sprinkler or soaker hoses before they go home so you only have to turn on the spigot. Soaker hoses are more efficient and waste less water than a sprinkler.

Deadhead as needed and as much as you are able. Then, when your annuals have stopped growing flowers, it will be time to change them out. Hopefully, the flowers will keep coming until the end of summer. But when it's time, you can get the family together again to change them out for fall flowers like mums.

All annuals don't have to be planted in the ground. If you live in an apartment or townhouse, you can plant them in decorative containers and place them on your balcony, deck or patio. Be sure to use lightweight containers like plastic. And, if you plan to move them around a lot, you can get wheeled dollies to put them on.

As an alternative to making the spring planting of annuals a family event, you can place containerized annuals in the planting bed. You can buy the plants in nursery pots rather than little six packs and slip the nursery pot into your decorative containers. To reduce the weight you have to carry, place the decorative container where you want to display the flowers and then slip the nursery pot into it. You can also plant annuals from a six pack into repurposed nursery pots and slip them into decorative containers. Be sure to use potting mix, not native soil from your garden.

The benefits of containerized annuals include not having to kneel, easy handling and the ability to move your annuals around during the growing season. The biggest downside is that they may have to be watered more often and they are more vulnerable to the elements because the roots are more exposed than those planted in the ground.

Follow these suggestions and you won't have to give up the beauty and fragrance of annual flowers. All you have to do is adapt.

SHRUBS VS PERENNIALS

*P*erennials are popular but senior gardeners should think twice before planting them. Consider shrubs instead. Shrubs require less maintenance and are easier to care for.

In her book, *Gardening for a Lifetime*, the late Sydney Eddison wrote that she ripped the perennials out of her garden and replaced them with shrubs. So did Marcy Klein (see photo above), a senior gardener in Rochester, NY. You would think that perennials would be the better choice for Seniors but they tend to spread and have to be divided, some annually. That takes a lot of heavy work. You have to dig the plant out of the ground, carry or drag it to a suitable location, and cut the roots into quarters. That can be a very difficult job if the roots are really large and knarly. Once split, you'll need to plant each quarter.

Usually, one quarter of a divided perennial is replanted into the hole from which it came. The other three may be planted on other sites in your garden or given to friends or charity plant sales. You have to do something with the roots of those other three sections. That means either wrapping them in burlap or planting them in a container for transport to their new homes.

These tasks don't even include deadheading. In addition to deadheading, some herbaceous perennials have to be cut back each fall when the leaves and stems turn a crispy brown.

After planting, a shrub needs only occasional pruning, if any. And, depending on your soil conditions, it may need occasional fertilizing, too. Shrubs grow in a wide variety of shapes and sizes. Some are dwarf*. Many are conifers that exhibit year round color and texture. Some shrubs can be shaped, although once you shape a shrub, you have to trim it regularly to keep the shape. Even deciduous shrubs can be interesting in winter. With the leaves off, some show off colorful stems and branches.

Simplicity is one of the goals of senior gardeners as they adapt. Replacing labor intensive perennials with shrubs that require less work is one good way to meet this goal. After all, perennials are in flower for only a short period every season. The rest of the time, they are green foliage plants like most shrubs.

*When buying dwarf conifers, be sure to check the tags or ask a garden center horticulturist about their maximum height and spread. The dwarf version of a 50 or 60 foot tree may grow to 25 or 30 feet. Be sure that's what you want before you buy.

WHAT'S SO GREAT ABOUT NATIVE PLANTS
FOR SENIOR GARDENERS?

*N*ative plants are all the rage these days. Some gardeners wouldn't think of planting anything else. Others aren't quite so adamant. I'm one of those. There are a lot of introduced varieties that have taken to their new environments and grown nicely without any problems. Today, we even have a new group of plants called "nativars." These are cultivars of native plants.

There is a distinct advantage to native plants, especially for senior gardeners. They tend to require less maintenance than introduced species. They've developed ways to resist native insects and diseases. I qualify that because they are still at the mercy of introduced pests like the emerald ash borer. Native plants also grow predictably in their native environment, unlike some non-native plants that may become so happy that they spread like wildfire and become invasive. Native plants also are attractive to pollinators. Bees, butterflies and birds that have been coming to native species for eons may be put off by introduced species that aren't appetizing to them.

Sometimes, the definition of native and non-native plants get blurred a bit. Over the centuries, some plants have grown just fine in their adopted homes. They behave themselves and don't spread out and become invasive. Pollinators have tried them and liked them, and they have developed natural pest repellents. When I say that these plants have been here for centuries, I mean that, in colonial times, there was brisk trade in plants between England and the United States. Many plants considered native today were actually brought here by settlers or were traded among early nurserymen like Thomas Jefferson and John Bartram.

So, why should you stick with native plants? Because they have a history – a track record. When you buy them and plant them, you can be pretty sure that they'll stay within bounds and not break out and become invasive. You can be quite confident that their only insect and disease problems will be limited to those listed in any literature on the plants. It's a much safer bet that you'll be planting the right plant in the right place, and the result will be less work for you, simplifying your senior gardening.

The photo from my front yard (on the previous page) shows the consequences of not practicing what I preach. The foundation plants on the left include a Japanese red maple and English boxwoods, as well as a couple of PJM rhododendrons. On the right are Korean lilacs and a spirea. The boxwoods and lilacs have to be sheared or pruned every year after they've finished adding new growth. While the Japanese red maple looks like it's getting out of hand, it hadn't had a real, professional pruning since it was planted in 2002. It had its first haircut shortly after the photos were taken. The only maintenance needed in the post lamp garden is cutting back the ornamental grass and dead phlox stems each spring.

VARY YOUR GARDENING TASKS, TAKE FREQUENT BREAKS

*R*emember when you were younger and could spend the whole day doing a single task in the garden? It may have involved preparing the garden or planting. But you shouldn't do that today.

Back in the day, you could spend the whole day on your knees planting. When you looked in the mirror, you probably had sun burn and thought nothing of it. I doubt if you'd spend a whole day on your knees in the sun again, considering how you feel and what you know today. Besides the toll age has taken on your body, medical research has found that prolonged exposure to direct sunlight is dangerous for your health. In addition to potential for skin cancer, working in sunlight without protection can also exacerbate conditions like macular degeneration.

You can still spend time in the garden but pace yourself. Work at one task for a short period of time – say an hour – and then go into a cool, shady spot for 20 or 30 minutes. Rest with a nice, cold drink of water. Then return to work at a different job and continue to practice this variable routine until you start to tire and then call it a day. Not till you drop but when you begin to feel tired.

Besides the pacing of your work, don't forget the sunscreen, wide brim hat and sunglasses. Protect yourself against disease carrying insects like ticks and mosquitoes, too. That means wearing a long sleeve shirt, long pants, and socks. Tuck your shirt in and, if possible, tuck your pants inside your socks. When you get back in the house after gardening, check your skin to be sure there are no ticks. If there are, remove them with a pair of tweezers.

Gardening in your later years means gardening smarter. Don't do strenuous work for an extended period and vary your tasks. Take frequent rest and refreshment breaks. Protect yourself against insects and the sun. And, you can continue to enjoy gardening, hopefully for a good many years to come.

HIRE OTHERS WHEN YOU CAN'T DO IT YOURSELF

*Y*ou'll probably need help simplifying your garden, depending on how much has to be done. Upon completion, see what it takes to tend your simplified, downsized garden. If it becomes too much for you, begin looking for help for maintenance tasks.

If your area doesn't have an abundance of gardeners, it might be a good idea to begin the search process now. Put out feelers among your gardening friends. Check social media and classified ads in your local newspapers and shopping guides. You might even interview candidates for the position and, if you find a good fit, hire them for certain tasks but retain those tasks you still want to do, and are still able to do.

I have always hired my local landscape client to do the major work like lawn care, Plant Health Care, tree work and planting of everything except annuals. This company doesn't mow or weed beds, so I went looking for a mower and a gardener.

Finding a mower was difficult because most don't want to get off their zero turn mowers. My lawn, however, is small and curvy with tight turns. Zero turn mowers can rip up the lawn on turns that tight. I wanted to find someone who has a walk behind mower and isn't afraid to use it.

Finding someone to weed and maintain the beds was more difficult. Our upstate New York community just doesn't have people who work exclusively as gardeners. They're all landscapers. When I found the right mowing guy, however, I learned that he is trained as a landscaper and was willing to do my weeding, so I hired him.

Don't be a martyr! When the body tells you that it's time to give it a rest, leave the work you can no longer do to a younger, stronger professional. There's no shame in that. You'll be a happier gardener, rather than an achy, curmudgeony gardener.

You don't have to be bedridden to have mobility problems. Do what you can and hire a good gardening partner to do the rest. Don't just hire the first person who comes along. Make sure you're on the same page, that you get along well and that he/she understands that you are a pair, that you'll be helping out where and when you can. Who knows, you may be making a good friend.

FINDING A GARDENER

*F*inding lawn care companies is easy compared to the problem many of us have finding a gardener in certain parts of the country. The best I could do for a photo is the statue of a gardener trimming a tree at Minter Gardens (now closed) near Vancouver, British Columbia Canada.

You'll have to do a little research to find out about the gardener market in your area. The best way to start is to check with any family or friends who retain gardeners. Perhaps your friends or neighbor's gardener has an opening and would be happy to gain another client.

Gardeners have a wide range of education, experience and skills. Some work for companies and some are self-employed. It's important to know the difference. A company will have a list of jobs they will do and the billing rate. Billing may be by the day, hour or season.

The self employed gardener may be very flexible. But it's important that you agree on the scope of the work, the times to be worked and the billing rate. It's important that you are familiar with the government's definition of an employee vs an independent contractor. This will keep you from becoming too demanding. When you dictate the hours and days a person will work, insist that they use your tools, and that they meet several other criteria, the government defines them as employees. Then you'll have to withhold and pay taxes, pay half the gardener's social security and keep careful records. I don't think you want to do that. You just want the gardener to show up at the agreed upon time, do the work and bill you.

I recommend that you insist on a certificate of insurance to protect yourself and any necessary licenses or certifications that your jurisdiction requires for both an individual and a company.

Some gardeners will do the lawn care work that I discussed in the last chapter, as well as light pruning. But don't let your gardener climb trees to prune. Hire a Certified Arborist for that dangerous job. Many gardeners stick only to planting bed maintenance. That's why it's best to define the scope of work, in writing, before retaining the gardener. Remember why you are retaining a gardener – to help you with those gardening tasks you are no longer able to do. You should be the final decision maker and, if you want to work with the gardener to any extent that you are able, that should all be part of the agreement.

I recently read the somewhat cynical comment that the way you can tell the difference between a gardener and landscaper is the gardener has dirty knees and the landscaper smells of gasoline. This means that a gardener does more light work that can be done with hand tools while the landscaper does heavier work in which power tools make the job much easier. Many landscapers can't afford to do the work of a gardener while others have set up separate divisions that do gardening for clients. That's why it's imperative that you do your due diligence.

You might also call a nearby college or university with an ornamental horticulture curriculum and see if they have any students who would like to work with you. If you go that route, treat the college student the same way you would a professional gardener who came to you by another route. Be sure both of you understand and agree on what's expected and the billing rate. You'll probably have to supply this person with a form 1099 at the end of the year, just as you do for any other unincorporated business you hire to do work. Check with your tax consultant.

BRING THE NEXT GENERATION
INTO THE GARDEN

This raised bed is in the Gardens on Spring Creek in Fort Collins, Colorado. Even public gardens introduce children to an early love of gardening by installing kids gardens.

As we adapt to our new gardening abilities and techniques, one that I've not seen mentioned is to bring the next generation into the garden. There's nobody better than you to instill the love of gardening in your children and grandchildren, and there's no better time to do it than right now.

You'll need different approaches for your children and grandchildren. Grown children may be somewhat set in their ways with their own interests and activities, which don't include gardening. Grandchildren, on the other hand, probably haven't formed interests yet. They may be experimenting with different activities like sports, Scouts or just sitting on the couch playing video games.

Many people take up gardening toward the end of the period called middle age. If your kids aren't gardeners now, make it your mission to introduce them to the enjoyment they can have by becoming gardeners. Besides the satisfaction of knowing that they're engaged in a good, healthy activity, gardening together is a way of spending quality time, as well as getting some much needed help without having to hire a gardener. Make gardening with your kids fun and, hopefully, they'll find it to be an activity they want to pursue. Plying them with nice, fresh produce won't hurt either. Eventually, they'll realize that this source of fresh food could dry up as you shrink your garden, and they'll take up the mantle. It may sound Pollyannaish but it's certainly worth a try.

Converting your children into gardeners will probably be more difficult than interesting your grandchildren. Grandchildren are more impressionable – like molding clay. Try asking them to garden with you but be sure to give them meaningful work like planting and harvesting. Don't just make them into weed pulling specialists. Training and supervising them may take more time and patience than you're used to but it'll be worth it.

Take your grandkids to the garden center when you go to buy your plants. Ask them to pick out one to be their very own plant to nurture and grow. Impress upon them that the veggies or flowers are theirs. When you get home, show them how to plant and care for their plant, and explain the benefits of plants.

A few years ago, garden trends surveys found that young adults like to be among plants and eat fresh fruits and vegetables but that they didn't have time to garden. More recently, this age group is investing in homes with smaller yards, including urban homes, and are doing great things with small space gardens. Small space gardens are also being recommended for senior gardeners. It's interesting that these gardens can be the answer to time and ability constraints on both ends of the age continuum.

Introducing your children and grandchildren to gardening now can give them a leg up on those who have had to learn about gardening on their own.

MAKING TOUGH DECISIONS
DECIDING WHETHER TO DOWNSIZE...OR NOT

*W*hen you start thinking about downsizing, you'll have a lot of choices from which to decide what is best for you. When making those decisions, consider the size of your gardens and lot, as well as the size of your house, and the ease of maintaining both.

One choice is moving from the large, two-story house on a large lot that you currently have to a smaller, one-story, single-family home on a small lot. Another is to consider a townhouse and a third is an apartment. If gardening is important to you, the smaller, one-story house on a small lot would likely be your best choice. That's what I did in 2001. Then you are free to keep the current landscaping, modify it to your taste or rip it all out and start fresh.

The photo above shows a small space garden in a small back yard. This space has everything – a tree, flowering plants, foliage plants, two big containers and even statues. I like this garden but my only concern is that there may be more maintenance than I'd care to do.

Townhouses and apartments offer fewer gardening options. Townhouse communities are usually governed by homeowners associations

(HOAs), which allow limited landscaping and gardening opportunities. In most cases, the HOA owns and maintains the common areas, including individual front and back yards. This means you probably can't plant around the foundation or plant a tree in your yard without the HOA's permission. However, most townhouses have decks or patios where you can put containerized plants. You also own the inside of your townhouse so you can raise any kind of houseplant you want.

Apartments are rental units so the landlord controls what you can grow both inside and out. Read the lease before you sign to be sure you are OK with any plant restrictions. You are probably free to grow any legal houseplants inside. If you have a balcony, you can probably grow anything that will fit. Just be sure you are familiar with any restrictions.

Downsizing to a townhouse or apartment will be a great opportunity to expand your indoor garden. The maintenance is also much easier on your body than outdoor, in-ground gardening.

As time goes on, assisted living may be in your future. If so, you'll probably be limited by space to only a few of your prized containerized plants. However, some centers offer gardening as one of their activities.

Regardless of your downsize choice, if you find the amount of gardening you can do is not enough, volunteer to teach gardening at a community organization. Besides giving you more time in the dirt, this activity will also train next generation gardeners.

GARDENING IN SMALL SPACES

Small space means different things to different people. To some, small space gardening may come in stages (i.e., from large lot to small lot to patio to balcony). This is the preferred method, in my opinion. It lets your green thumb fade gradually.

Speaking from personal experience, we downsized from a half acre lot to a quarter acre lot in 2001. The single story house we had built has about the same size footprint as the larger house. Outside, about a third of the property is a hill that we had excavated to the top and landscaped. Stone was installed in the drainage swale at the bottom of the hill so it resembles a dry riverbed most of the time. There is very little lawn in the back. Most of the space is a large, freeform, stamped concrete patio and landscaping. There is more lawn in the front but still plenty of landscaping. I just had an overgrown rock garden removed and replaced by an oval perennial garden. This resulted in a bit less grass.

This downsize cut my mowing time from an hour on a rider to 20 minutes with a walk behind. As the plants on the hill grew, I let nature take over and am happy with the results.

I'm hoping this is my forever home but if it isn't, I have plenty of houseplants to continue gardening.

If your downsize is to a townhouse, most have patios, which you can landscape. Some patios have privacy fences around them while others don't. You are usually free to landscape your patio area. If it isn't completely paved, you can plant in-ground. Otherwise, you can put out as many containerized plants as will fit.

Apartment dwellers may have a balcony on which to put a few containers. Crops most often mentioned are tomatoes and herbs. It would be nice if you could fill some containers with flowers or a foliage plant like a miniature evergreen tree or a dwarf shrub. Or better yet, create container gardens in which you plant a mixture of veggies and flower and/or foliage plants in the same container.

To keep from having to bend over to tend your containers, buy a tall pot made of a lightweight material like plastic faux terra cotta. Put a rock or two in the bottom to reduce the risk of the pot tipping over from being top heavy. Get planter inserts to "raise the floor" of the planter so you don't have to use so much potting mix. Then you can work standing up or sitting in a chair.

WHEN TO BECOME A FULL TIME
CONTAINER GARDENER

*Y*our body will answer the title question for you. When you can't kneel, stand or work for any length of time without getting short of breath, or when heat and sun wear you out. Any one or combination of these symptoms should be your first sign that you ought to stroll around the container department on your next trip to the garden center.

You'll probably have to psyche yourself into making this change. From the practical standpoint, get a gardener or landscaper to do the heavy, in-ground work. From the psychological standpoint, don't look upon in-ground gardening as one more thing you can no longer do. Rather, look upon container gardening as being on the cutting edge of a new gardening trend. Check out the photos of a patio (above) to see attractive container plantings.

The reason you'll find a big selection of decorative containers at the garden store is because people buy them. Read any gardening magazine and you'll find that containerized plants are all the rage, and they are easy to plant. You can do it sitting down or standing at a potting bench. I spread newspaper out on the kitchen table and pot up houseplants there. Outside plants are done either in the garage sitting in a lawn chair or at a bistro table on the patio. However, I don't do much potting for outside plants anymore. I simply buy plants in nursery pots that will just slip into the decorative container.

One other tip – buy lightweight containers made of plastic or fiberglass instead of ceramic or concrete. Place the decorative container where you want to display the plant that will go into it. Then place the plant in the container. This way you won't have to lug a heavy, awkward, full container. Check the plant for moisture and water if necessary. Don't over fertilize or you'll be replacing plants sooner than you expected. You will most likely have to water containerized plants more often than those planted in the ground.

If you live in the north, be prepared to take all but the hardiest containerized plants inside for the winter. Some can be used as houseplants, unless you already have a whole house full of houseplant, like me (see photo below). Except for a couple of yuccas, I limit my outdoor containerized plants to annuals. By the end of the season, they'll be ready for the trash and the containers get stacked in the garage for the winter. The yuccas overwinter at my significant other's house where they are as happy as me.

Finally, as we get older, a lot can be said about raising an extensive collection of houseplants. That's why I'll save that subject for another time. I will say, though, that you don't have to be bothered by the heat or cold in order to raise houseplants. They are just easier to handle as we grow older.

GET RID OF YOUR LAWN

A few years ago, the mere suggestion that you get rid of your lawn would be viewed as landscape heresy. Today, though, reducing or removing lawns is a key component of such movements as xeriscaping, sustainability and now, adaptive gardening.

Check out the photo above. This garden was on a Garden Writers Association (now GardenComm) tour in Portland, Oregon. In this case, the gardens in front of the house eliminate the need to mow the steep slopes, as well as benefit the environment.

Depending on where you live, your lawn requires water, fertilizer, insect control, weeding and mowing. It may also need occasional aeration and dethatching. That's about as far from sustainability as you can get, regardless of your age. When you get older, performing as simple a task as weekly mowing can be a real chore. Or an expense if you hire it out. As a senior citizen, you should have the best motivation to put lawn work behind you. Yet, it's the younger people – the millennials – who believe they have better things to do with their lives than spend every weekend mowing.

The one big question you may have is what to put in if you remove your grass. That depends on where you live. One of my sons and daughters-in-law live in Arizona and they have desert plants and stone in their front yard. Where I live in New York, that probably wouldn't go over well with the neighbors or the local code enforcement authorities.

You may want to keep a bit of lawn if you have a dog. My desert-dwelling kids do. But it doesn't have to be tended. It's fake.

In his book, *Slow Gardening*, garden writer Felder Rushing suggests reducing or eliminating grass if you want to reduce your gardening workload and enjoy your landscape more. A phrase he uses frequently is throw rug rather than wall-to-wall-carpeting. That means keeping a small patch of grass and converting the rest to meadow grass, ground cover, shrubs and/or trees.

If the thought of replacing your sod with the plants Felder Rushing suggests is hard to get your head around, engage a professional landscape designer. Removing sod and converting the space into planting beds is hard work. At your age, my advice is to also hire a professional landscape contractor to do the job. If your landscape designer works for the landscape contractor, you may not have to pay extra for the design.

SUSTAINABILITY – GOOD FOR THE ENVIRONMENT AND OUR SENIOR BODIES

*T*he gardening buzzword for today is "sustainability." You'll see the term used often in garden writing but what does it mean?

When I checked Google for the definition, it gave me 6,180,000 sites. So, I decided that the most authentic definition would be this one, put forth by the United Nations' Brundtland Report in 1987 – "… design, construction, operations and maintenance practices that meet the needs of the present without compromising the ability of future generations to meet their own needs."

I'm not a big buzzword of the month person but sustainability makes sense because it helps me attain my goal of low maintenance landscaping. Low maintenance because you aren't "helping" Mother Nature to the extent that many people think we should. After all, look at how much we've helped her so far.

Sustainable gardening is a set of practices that provides for your needs now and in the future. It's organic gardening to the extreme.

Sustainable gardening starts by applying the landscaper's mantra – right plant, right place." If a plant is happy in its environment, it will be healthier. It will attract fewer insects and diseases, requiring fewer pesticides. It will grow vigorously with less need for synthetic fertilizer. All of this is good for the environment as well as your health and vitality.

Speaking of vigor and vitality, the late, great plant physiologist, Dr. Alex Shigo, defines vigor as, "the genetically controlled capacity – potential – to survive after injury and infection." And vitality as, "the dynamic ability to grow and reproduce within the limits of vigor." So, when we speak of vigor, we often mean vitality.

The easiest way to a sustainable landscape is to stick with native plants, especially if you want to attract birds and wildlife. As I've mentioned before, I'm not an advocate of the "Native plants are the only plants" movement. However, if you want to be sure the plants you select will grow sustainably with minimal maintenance, and won't be invasive, the best idea is to stick with natives. Of course, you then have to hope that none of the foreign pests that are attacking native plants make it to your area.

Sustainability also means peacefully coexisting with weeds. Chemical herbicides aren't part of an organic gardener's toolbox. As we get older, pulling weeds by hand gets tougher and tougher on the body. Except, maybe, for my father. He would go out with his little stool and a weed digger well into his 70s. I think it was therapeutic for him. But for most of us, it's a chore. Installing plants close together is one sustainable technique for discouraging weeds.

Some other sustainable practices include planting to attract pollinators. That involves planning and planting for their habitat needs. Finally, don't plant during the heat of summer or you'll have to use a lot of water. Instead, plant after temperatures begin cooling down and the rains return in late August or early September. Remember, Fall is for Planting.

Sustainability isn't limited to plants. It also extends to hardscapes. Recycle, reuse and repurpose rather than investing in new plastic hardscape items. Hit garage sales rather than home centers to see what they have that can be reused or repurposed.

Sustainability sounds almost like conservation, doesn't it? The definition of conservation, however, is "the wise use of our natural resources." Sustainability goes beyond that definition to include supporting ecological balance.

TIME FOR LAWN CARE DECISIONS

Spring begins officially in March. Although March can be pretty wintery in some parts of the country, it can be very spring like in others. That means you'll soon have to begin caring for your lawn, if you still have lawn.

Lawn care is about as personal as any gardening or landscaping decisions. Everyone eventually has to decide when to stop doing it themselves. Some people, regardless of age, enjoy mowing their own lawns. Some find it very relaxing to ride around on a lawn mower each weekend. At some point, however, hiring a mowing service will make more sense. When the summer heat starts getting to you, hiring it out will be a wise decision. If ragged stripes reveal that your vision and/or coordination aren't as sharp as it was, that should be another hint.

Then there are decisions concerning fertilization and weed and insect control. While some people today refuse to use any chemicals in their gardens, others still apply at least fertilizer once or twice a season. Many still strive to conquer broadleaf weeds like dandelions. When you do it yourself, these tasks can build up a real sweat. That's why so many lawn services are in business. It is often less expensive to hire a lawn service than to buy the material and spread it yourself, never mind what it does to your aging body.

Lawn care is, arguably, the easiest landscape task to give up. Turning the job over to professionals with their specialized equipment leaves you with more time and energy to undertake less routine tasks that are really more fun.

When shopping for a lawn care company, resign yourself to the fact that you will probably have to hire two companies – one to mow and one to apply fertilizer and weed/insect control. In some rare instances, you may find one company that does it all. If so, congratulations.

Lawn mowing companies have specific routes for their crews and have determined exactly how long it should take to mow each lawn. They arrive, quickly mow, trim, blow away the clippings, and are off to the next property. That's why they are referred to as mow. blow and go guys in the landscape industry.

The companies that apply fertilizers and pest control products are specialists in that phase of lawn care. In most, if not all states, they have to be licensed to apply pesticides commercially. This requires study, examinations and continuing education to maintain their licenses.

Both types of lawn care professionals have their specialty and their business model so that's why you should expect to need two lawn care companies to care for your lawn. But, take it from me: it's so worth it.

MAKING LESS DIFFICULT DECISIONS

TRY SLOW GARDENING AS YOU AGE

*M*y grandmother was never one to hold back when she had an opinion. After one such proclamation, I remember her saying, "I'm 80 years old so I can say anything I damn please." It's the same way with gardening. You can plant anything you damn please, as long as it'll grow in your area without a lot of maintenance.

There's even a name for that, thanks to garden writer Felder Rushing. He calls it *Slow Gardening*. I highly recommend his book (see cover above) by the same name, which is available wherever books are sold.

Slow gardening is a relaxed approach to gardening – a great way for us seniors to adapt to our advancing physical limitations. Put aside the rules and plant what you want, wear what you want, garden when you want and lay out the garden the way you want. It's not written in stone anywhere that you have to plant in straight rows. If you want to plant in concentric circles, do it. From what I've read and seen in pictures, Felder Rushing is the consummate slow gardener.

The locavore movement is an example of slow gardening. Locavores source as much of their food locally as possible, including some from their own back yards. This leads to sustainability (another buzz word) without even having to think about it.

Felder wrote that, "You don't have to be an expert to garden, or even to work very hard. Even a small potted plant can help you focus on the 'here and now' of everyday living."

Slow gardeners focus on seasonal rhythms and local conditions. I must admit that I backslid. I had my landscape client remove a long, narrow rock garden from my front yard and replace it with an oval perennial garden, and plant new grass around it. My usual laid-back approach became a bit uptight about keeping the new lawn watered. Luckily, the good Lord had my back. He sent plenty of rain, lessening the waterings that I had to worry about.

If you've been following my blog, slow gardening should be nothing new. I've been writing about it since Day One. Now, I've wrapped it into a neat package, tied it with a bow and shared its name.

ATTRACTING BUTTERFLIES & BIRDS
TO YOUR SENIOR GARDEN

*A*ccording to all I've read in the trade press, we seniors enjoy having birds and butterflies visit our gardens. This pleases Mother Nature, too. You may have heard that the pollinator population is dropping dramatically and researchers haven't found a reason for this drop.

Butterflies are good pollinators, as are certain birds like hummingbirds. But bees are still the best pollinators. Be forewarned that planting to attract pollinators will bring bees right along with the butterflies and hummingbirds. You can't discriminate.

Pollinators like plants with large, colorful flowers. Many pollinators also like flowers with long "throats." You can recognize these flowers because their reproductive parts are deep into the flower. You have to peer down into the flower to see them. The pollinators that like these flowers are those with a long proboscis (the nectar-sucking mouthparts).

Nectar is the food pollinators want. As they are gathering nectar, they pick up pollen on their feet. When they fly to another plant for more nectar, they deposit the pollen from their feet and pick up more from that plant.

When you buy plants, the nursery tags should indicate whether they attract pollinators. If they don't, talk to one of the horticulturists at your local garden center.

While flowers attract pollinators, there is another part of the equation. You also have to supply food for the butterfly larvae (caterpillars). It's common knowledge that milkweed is monarch butterfly caterpillars' only food source. Other species prefer dill and fennel. Again, check with a horticulturist at your local garden center to find out what your local pollinator larvae like.

Besides food, you also need to supply pollinators with water and shelter. A birdbath is fine for larger pollinators but butterflies may prefer a puddler. A puddler is a stone with an indentation for the water. They are available at garden stores and online. Or you can make your own. It's like a tiny birdbath so butterflies can drink without drowning. For shelter, install birdhouses and butterfly houses for those pollinators. Birdbaths and bird feeders will also attract songbirds.

When placing birdhouses, keep in mind that some birds remove the waste from their nests and jettison it as soon as they get airborne so you may not want your birdhouse too close to your patio.

My last advice on attracting pollinators and birds is to keep it as simple or make it as fancy as you want and can afford.

INCLUDE EDIBLES IN YOUR SENIOR GARDEN

Can you find the tomatoes growing in this flower garden?

Were you brought up eating fresh vegetables? I wasn't. We usually had canned vegetables. Occasionally, we would enjoy a salad. Today, nutritionists and gardeners alike are emphasizing the health benefits of fresh, naturally grown vegetables.

For some of us, eating fresh, organic veggies is a whole new learning experience. Learning to grow our own vegetables can be yet another learning experience. But it doesn't have to be traumatic. If you have the space, plant a vegetable garden. Veggies grow well in raised beds. Some crops can be started from seeds, which are sold in garden centers in little packets. Each packet has planting instructions printed on it. Just follow them. Other crops like tomatoes, peppers, cucumbers and onions are best planted from already germinated plants that you buy at the garden store. Tomatoes, peppers and cucumbers are vines that need a trellis or something to climb in order to keep the fruit off the ground. The easiest prop is a wire frame that you can buy at the garden center.

If you don't have room for raised beds dedicated to growing veggies, mix vegetable plants right in with your flowers. No, you won't be considered weird. You'll be fashionable. Integrated vegetable and flower gardens are one of the up and coming gardening trends. After all, veggie plants flower before they set fruit, so they'll fit right in.

If you only garden in containers, no problem. You can still mix herbs and flowers in the same container. If the pot is big enough, you can plant a tomato plant right in the center and flowering annuals all around it. When the flowering plants have lived their life, you can replace them with late summer flowering annuals and then pick the nice, red, juicy tomatoes.

Sweet corn is the only crop that's difficult to integrate into a flower bed, unless the flowers are sunflowers. Corn pretty much needs a bed of its own. But there's nothing to say you can't plant it in raised beds. Don't let corn's height intimidate you. Plant it somewhere, even if it's along the fence line.

It's never too late to get healthy. If convention was holding you back, now's your chance to try your hand at growing veggies. There are no longer any hard and fast rules governing gardening in general and veggie gardening specifically, so give it a try. If you have questions, call your local extension office. Every state has a Master Gardener program, and their graduates staff phones to answer questions just like yours.

INTRODUCE WHIMSY INTO YOUR GARDEN

A bit of whimsy can lighten the garden work by making it even more fun to be outdoors. I can't tell you how to incorporate whimsy into your garden, however. It's all a matter of your personal taste and your sense of humor. The whimsy in your garden may be as simple as an interesting garden gnome or it may be an imaginative repurposing of old, rusty garden tools. Like planting flowers in an old wheelbarrow.

Garden whimsy can be done with hardscape or garden art, or you can use interesting plant arrangements. Or use a combination of all of them. The main thing is to be natural. Let what you choose reflect your sense of humor. Don't let it be forced or you won't have any fun with it.

If your personality is more serious, consider a garden railroad or nice pieces of garden art. Whimsy is endearing quaintness or oddity. So, rather than looking for something that's quirky that doesn't fit your personality, look for something that just says, "I need that in my garden."

The basket containing three giant eggs (see photo above) in a garden in North Carolina really caught my eye. I'd love to have one like it in my garden so I could have fun telling people they're dinosaur eggs.

One word of caution: Be sure your whimsical stuff doesn't add more work and increase maintenance. Because then it won't be fun anymore. I have some cast concrete statues that are mighty heavy. These days, I have had to enlist the help of a son or grandson each fall to take them to the garage for winter storage and to bring them out again in the spring. For the last two years, however, I've left them in place with a big garbage bag over them with duct tape holding the bags in place, and they've done just fine.

Gardening is intended to be a relaxing pastime. We may be getting older, but we don't have to lose our sense of humor. We may get down on ourselves when we come across tasks we can't do without help. That's when turning around and seeing something that tickles our funny bone makes the acceptance of our limitations easier. The best laughs are when we laugh at ourselves.

A CAUTION ABOUT BUYING FIREWOOD

*T*his caution is for anyone who buys firewood for a fire pit, fireplace, wood burning stove or other appliance that uses cord wood. Be careful of where, and from whom, you buy your firewood. Firewood is the major transportation vehicle for invasive insects like the dreaded emerald ash borer, Asian longhorned beetle, gypsy moth, spotted lanternfly and more.

Emerald ash borer, for example, lives most of its life inside a tree, feasting on the phloem (the food made by photosynthesis and the vessels that transport it). As a result, it can't be seen until the adult emerges and begins flying. Then it's too late.

The gypsy moth and spotted lanternfly lay their eggs in egg sacs on the trunk and branches. This is how they hitchhike to new locations. The point is that hitchhiking insects can travel across many states to establish new frontiers. And there are unscrupulous firewood dealers who help them do it.

Laws are in effect prohibiting wood products from being transported more than 50 miles from the wood's place of origin without certification that the wood is insect-free. Insect-free means the wood has gone through a special process to kill the insects. Places where these insects are active have been quarantined, which means wood can't be moved outside of the quarantine zone.

It's hard to resist a bargain but, in this case, the cost to have a large tree removed and replaced from your yard, killed by imported, deadly pests, far outweighs any money you saved on firewood.

It's best to buy locally from a firewood dealer that you know. If you don't have any dealers who buy their wood locally, ask the right questions before you buy from a stranger. Insist on seeing government documentation certifying that the wood is insect-free. It may cost a few bucks more but it could save you thousands in tree removal costs.

SENIOR GARDENING THROUGH THE SEASONS

NEW YEARS RESOLUTIONS FOR THE GERIATRIC GARDENER

*I*f you're a geriatric gardener who hasn't modified your approach to gardening yet, this would be a good time to do so. It's the time of year when we all make resolutions designed for a new year that's better than the old one. Even though the bubbly's gone and the horns and hats put away for another year, you can still make resolutions. When you make them is secondary to whether you keep them.

The Ohio State University's Cooperative Extension has published a factsheet full of tips for the gardener with physical limitations. They are separated by these subheads for easy reference:

• Simple Gardening Style Changes

• Protecting Joints When Gardening and Preventing Overexertion

• Assistive Technology for the Garden

• Alternative Garden Types

• Choosing the Right Tool for the Job.

We've covered many of the OSU tips in previous chapters but there are others that I never thought of like:

• Avoid tasks requiring gripping for extended periods of time and wear high-quality gripping gloves to protect your hands and improve dexterity. This applies to people like me who have knarly, arthritic, sausage fingers.

• Complete more physically demanding tasks early in the day. Not only will it be easier on you physically to get the demanding tasks done when you are still refreshed from a good night's sleep but you won't be doing these things in the hot, afternoon sun.

• Wearing a carpenter's apron helps keep track of gardening tools, requiring less bending. Makes good sense to me.

- Use ergonomic handled tools or tools with extended handles. I was in a mega garden center recently that had a whole department devoted to these tools.

- Garden seeders are readily available. There are several variations to meet specific needs with syringe-type dispensers and trowels with seed dispensers. I never thought of this because I never plant from seed.

The OSU site is bookmarked on my computer and I often refer to it. I hope you will take the opportunity to use your winter wisely and prepare to greet spring with the new you…the you who is ready to garden despite your physical limitations.

START PLANNING YOUR GARDEN IN WINTER

*Y*es, the last growing season has just ended but I have to ask you this question: Do you have any plans for making changes to your garden next year? Whether you are thinking of minor changes or a completely new landscape, you can use this downtime to plan just what you want to do, and can afford to do.

While the wind and snow cover your garden, you can be snuggled up in your house considering your various options. As you plan for plantings and any other renovations, be sure to consider any adaptive measures you may need as well.

Why renovate? Gardens need change year to year just as we do. And speaking of you, it may be necessary to make compromises to the plan you are mulling over in order to accommodate any new adaptive needs. For example, you may need to re-lay out your beds so they can be reached easily from the path. Then you can sit on a stool or garden cart while tending them. If you are going to raised beds, construction can begin indoors in winter. Then you'll be ready to get started outdoors as soon as spring begins peeking up from the ground.

On a cold, snowy , winter day, nothing beats curling up on the couch with a nice, hot beverage as a fire roars in the fireplace. Plant catalogs make good reading at these times. Makes you think of spring. However, as you check catalogs for new plant offerings, be sure to check each one's maintenance needs, too. Be sure they aren't high maintenance and difficult for you to provide proper care.

You may want to consider working with a professional designer. If possible, select a designer who has adaptive garden design experience. They will be able to advise you on measures that you need to take to provide proper care now and in the future.

Even if you hadn't planned to make changes to your garden but find you need to make more compromises to accommodate the aging process, you may want to consult with a landscape designer. They can recommend minor modifications to your garden to accommodate your changing physical limitations. Starting the planning process now will give you plenty of time to have everything ready to be implemented in the spring, and you won't miss a beat when the season begins.

Geriatric Gardener Survival Kit: Brimmed hat, sunscreen, medical alert and water.

*I*n the last chapter, I suggested getting a head start on planning your garden. Now I'm suggesting that you take stock in yourself. Things change over the winter. How are you adapting?

While I concentrated on raised beds in that last chapter, I'm making other recommendations today. Begin by jotting down your gardening goals for the coming season. Not what you're going to plant or which beds you're going to renovate but, rather, how much work you want to do in the garden this year and whether you have new challenges to meet. And what you need to meet those goals and challenges. For example...

- Be sure you have your survival kit – hat, water, emergency call device, sunglasses and sunscreen. (Pictured above)

- Do you have a mobility appliance that you didn't have last season? That could be a walker, wheelchair or even a garden seat. Then wider paths should probably be on your list. (Pictured next page top)

- Is your eyesight, hearing or memory fading? Then, perhaps, you need garden art that emits a sound or has bright colors to help orient you, depending on your impairment. Or you may need to highlight familiar landmarks within the garden to keep you from getting lost or disoriented. (Pictured next page center)

- Were tools heavier or more difficult to grip last fall than they were earlier last season. Then you may want to check out some of the new lightweight tools with foam grips. (Pictured next page bottom)

- Do you have plenty of cool places to sit and rest scattered around the garden? (Below right)

- Did things get heavier to carry and move around toward the end of last season? Then you may need a helper.

Mothers Day and Fathers Day are coming up. Hint broadly enough and maybe what you need may appear. If that's not possible, make the investment in what you need now so you'll be ready to hit the dirt as soon as it's dry enough. This will eliminate adding frustration to the other issues you have to deal with.

SENIOR GARDENING IN SUMMER

*Y*ou've simplified your senior garden and it's summer. What's a gardener to do now? That's simple. Enjoy it!

Sit on your porch, patio or deck, as Linda and I are doing in the photo, and just take in the results of your labor. There are a few things you can do when you get antsy from just sitting.

Water if the plants need it. If nature hasn't provided an inch of rain that week, your plants would probably like a drink. Hopefully, you've set up a network of soaker hoses so all you have to do is turn on the spigot and return to your seat while you watch the water ooze out of the hoses.

Soaker hoses take quite a while to deposit an inch of water. After all, you only turn the water on about a quarter turn or you risk blowing out the porous rubber hose walls.

You can deadhead spent flowers. This is also known as pinching them, although it's OK to use pruning shears if the flowers don't like being pinched. Removing spent flowers may encourage the plant to bloom again, rather than dropping seeds.

If you have a vegetable garden, you have an opportunity to perform a very pleasurable task – harvesting summer crops.

Any lawn you still have has probably turned a straw like yellowish brown. Don't worry. It'll green up again when the temperature moderates and the rain returns. Grass knows how to spend its summer, just as you should. Sit, relax, enjoy a cool drink and take in the season. If you live in upstate New York like me, this weather will be gone soon enough, and we'll wonder where it went.

Sitting and relaxing with a cool beverage can slow summer's swift passage considerably.

HOW TO RELAX & ENJOY YOUR SUMMER

Are your plans to sit outside with a cool drink enjoying the environment you've created? Or working up a sweat taking care of that environment?

If you would like the former but feel locked in to the latter, I have three words for you – Tend, don't toil! In other words, simplify your garden.

In her book, *Gardening for a Lifetime*, the late Sydney Eddison described how she simplified her garden by pulling out the perennials and replacing them with compact and dwarf shrubs. She explained how these shrubs require less care than perennials.

Compact and dwarf conifers include such plants as small, rounded boxwood and dwarf conifers like Alberta spruce and rounded top blue spruce (see photo on next page). I like these, too, and have a number in my yard, which is where the photos were taken.

These shrubs need little or no care. I've never had to prune my blue spruces but my compact boxwoods need a light pruning each year to maintain their shape. Herbaceous perennials, on the other hand, need pruning and dividing. Some grow so fast they need to be divided annually. Dividing perennials can be very difficult for the older gardener. I've dug up perennial roots that are really thick and a chore to cut, even for a younger gardener.

Trees are also good senior plants. Ornamentals grow shorter, and often showier, than shade trees. If you do plant trees, check with the horticulturist where you buy them to be sure they don't drop a lot of litter on the ground for you to clean up.

Leaves are another story. Deciduous trees and shrubs are going to drop their leaves. Sydney Eddison wrote that she just blew them back under shrubs so they'll decompose and return nutrients to the soil. You can do this with trees, too, but don't let the leaves pile up against the tree trunks or shrub stems. Leaves hold moisture, which can seep into any cracks in the bark. This is where rot starts. The leaves also provide cover for field mice and other small critters to chew on the tree or shrub bark when they get very hungry in winter. They can completely girdle the trunk and kill the tree.

Trees will probably need periodic pruning but you're not going to prune them yourself, are you? Please don't. Hire a certified arborist to do the job instead. They have the skill and the eye to do it right, the education to do it safely and the equipment to do it quickly.

Relaxing in the summer heat is good for your plants as well as your aging body. You may have to water and deadhead flowers but heavier tasks like fertilizing, elective pruning and other sweat generating chores should be put off until fall. For your health and the health of your plants

TIME FOR SLOW GARDENING SENIOR STYLE

Summer is a time to enjoy your garden rather than working in it. With all this time you'll have when you stop working and enjoying the season, you'll have plenty of time to think about how you garden – how you gardened in the past, how you garden today and how you'll garden in the future.

May I suggest that you give some thought to adopting slow gardening principles to your way of gardening in the present so you can continue on the slow gardening path in the years to come?

Slow gardening is a relaxed approach to gardening – a great way for us seniors to adapt to our advancing physical limitations. Put aside the rules and plant what you want, wear what you want, garden when you want and lay out the garden the way you want. If you want to hold off weeding for a couple of days, go ahead. They'll still be there when you get around to it. If you want to plant tomatoes right outside your kitchen door, go ahead. Who cares whether there's a flower garden there now? They'll all share the space. And, for a little fragrance and culinary convenience, why not plant some herbs there, too?

The whole idea of adaptive gardening is to make it so easy that you can continue to garden, despite the ravages of advancing years. The key is to simplify your garden. If maintenance is getting burdensome, identify the burdens and get rid of them.

Replacing perennials with shrubs, especially those planted close together, can reduce the need to weed. The closeness of the shrubs will reduce the sunlight that weeds love. Even if weeds do grow, they'll hardly be noticeable. Don't worry about them, you'll probably be the only one who knows they're there. Embracing imperfection is another credo of adaptive gardening.

I could go on and on but I hope you get the point. Besides, the patio beckons, so I'll leave you with one last thought. *Slow Gardening* author Felder Rushing lives in Mississippi where summers are really hot so he's sure to know what he was talking about when he wrote the book.

USE AUTUMN TO SIMPLIFY YOUR GARDEN

"Simplify" is the senior gardener mantra, and this autumn is a good time to start, or continue, the simplification process. Many of the simplification steps are fall tasks anyway. Just remember to take it easy and get help.

Removing roving perennials is one of the first steps to simplification, and fall is a good time to dig up your high maintenance perennials. This is a job that could use some help from family or your professional gardener. The last time I had to do this job, my son the nurseryman was in town.

Digging the plant out of the ground and cutting the roots into four sections isn't an easy job for us but it should be a breeze for someone several decades younger. The only way this final splitting will differ from previous divisions is that all four sections will be given away, rather than the customary three.

Fall is for planting, so the next step is to replace your perennials with shrubs that behave themselves, as was done in the photo above. First, research shrubs you are considering for perennial replacements. You don't want to replace one high maintenance plant with another. You should also decide whether you want flowering shrubs or foliage shrubs. Where are you going to plant them? Near hardscape like sidewalks, driveway or patio? If so, consider the amount of dropped flower petals you'll have to clean up.

As much as I like flowering shrubs, the flowers last for only a short period every year. They are foliage plants for the rest of the year, so I opt for foliage plants rather than clean up.

Fall is such a beautiful season. Enjoy it in the garden and take one more step toward minimal maintenance. Keep these two points in mind as you plan your fall gardening: Remember during this process that simplifying your landscape is goal number one and, don't schedule more work than you are up to in any one session.

FALL CLEANUP SENIOR STYLE

*F*all cleanup can be one of the most wonderful days of your life or it can be a day or more of pure drudgery. Jobs like raking or blowing leaves, fertilizing, winterizing containerized plants, and even picking up debris can tucker you out. If you have to do it yourself, it's best to spread it over several days with lots of rest in between. That's why I vote for making it a family get together.

Turn the workday into a social event. Have a cookout or just get pizza and wings. You can do the fun stuff while your kids and grandkids handle the tiring stuff for you.

It would be best if you schedule your yard cleaning party after the leaves have all fallen. That way, they'll only have to rake or blow once. What they do with the leaves depends on how your community handles them. Some let you rake or blow them to the curb and the town, village or city sucks them up with a big vacuum and takes them to the municipal composting facility. Others leave it up to individual property owners to maintain their own compost piles. Regardless, recycling is best for your yard and for the whole environment.

Everyone has their own idea on how to best handle leaves. Mine was pure labor in my younger days, and my compost wasn't that good because the leaves weren't chopped up sufficiently. The year we moved into our newly built house with no trees yet, I saw a TV garden show host put the leaves in a plastic trash can and plunge his string trimmer into the leaves repeatedly until they were tiny pieces. What a great idea!

Other jobs your family can help you with includes applying fertilizer to the lawn and any other plants that need it. Horticulturists are divided on the wisdom of fall fertilization. Some say that it helps plants make the food they need to sustain them through the winter, while others believe it's unnecessary. To fertilize or not to fertilize is a decision you'll have to make.

Your crew should also pick up debris that has accumulated and deter critters from making your yard their winter buffet.

If you're willing to host a cleanup party and your family is good with helping you out this way, you may have a new entry in your book of memories. Hopefully, you'll have so much fun that they'll ask you in the middle of summer, "When are we going to have our fall fun day?"

PUTTING YOUR LAWN TO BED

*I*f you're still mowing your lawn yourself, there are a few things you should do to minimize winter damage before putting the mower away for the winter.

During the season, you, hopefully, have been mowing to the recommended height of 3 to 4 inches. This height gives the grass leaves plenty of surface area to absorb sunlight for photosynthesis. Mowing high also encourages deeper roots and thicker turf. In winter, however, the taller turf can mat down from the weight of the snow, encouraging attacks by winter fungal diseases.

A preventive is to lower your mower's deck height to approximately 2 inches for the last mowing of the season. If you mow at the lower height and it turns out that grass keeps growing and needs additional mowings, continue to mow at the lower height for the remainder of the season.

If you use a lawn mowing service, be sure the person who mows your lawn knows that you want it short for the last mowing(s) of the season.

If you apply fertilizer and weed killer to your lawn, many agronomists recommend an early fall application of fertilizer and pre-emergent broadleaf weed killer. Fertilizer is recommended to replenish the soil nutrients the grass plants have used to make food all through the growing season. The plants need these nutrients to make plenty of food to sustain them through the winter.

Toward the end of the growing season, weeds dropped seeds into the turf, and other seeds have blown in from neighboring yards or were dropped by birds. Applying pre-emergent weed killer in the fall will keep those seeds from germinating in the spring. As you've probably noticed, weeds start growing while the grass is still dormant. If you have a lawn service, applying these materials in early fall is usually part of your contract.

If putting your lawn to bed made you want to hit the sack, a good winter project may be to research ways in which you can replace your lawn with ground cover or low maintenance planting beds next spring. Replacing your lawn can be good for your health and the health of the environment.

OVERWINTERING YOUR CONTAINERIZED PLANTS

Many senior (and non-senior) gardens are comprised of more and more containerized plants. While they take up less space and require less work during the growing season, care has to be taken to prepare them for winter. The method and extent depends on the climate where you live.

Annuals in your containers will be dead by the time the cold weather takes hold so they will end up on the compost heap or in the trash. It's the perennials and dwarf shrubs that you need to overwinter.

Plants that are hardy in your USDA hardiness zone can be left in place. For extra protection, it's recommended that you insulate the container because the plant roots are more exposed than they are in the ground. The soil around in-ground plants is usually insulation enough but most container material like ceramic or plastic isn't a very good insulator. Terra cotta won't survive freezing temperatures but, hopefully, your terra cotta pots are actually lightweight plastic.

Containerized plants on your deck or patio can be wrapped with material like bubble wrap, Styrofoam or burlap, and plastic wrapped to protect the insulating material. If you place your plants in containers in their nursery pots, you can also consider getting large, lightweight plastic pots and placing the plant, in its nursery pot, into the large pot surrounded by soil or mulch between the two pots and then putting a layer of mulch on top of the soil. You can then take the decorative pots inside out of harm's way for the winter. It is also recommended that you group the winterized containers in an area of your patio or deck that allows the plants to enjoy the sun and precipitation while being sheltered from the wind.

For containerized plants that live in your planting beds, burying them in a mound of mulch is a good idea. This is the only time that "mulch volcanoes" are good for plants. Some garden centers and online garden supply houses can make winterizing really easy with manufactured insulation products if you'd rather not use one of the DIY methods suggested here.

More tender plants would do best in a cold frame. These can be made from scratch or from kits available at the usual outlets for gardening products. Some sources have them already made and some even have tent-like folding cold frames (see photo on previous page).

Cold frames should be opened up on sunny days and the plants should be watered when the temperature climbs above freezing. Consider that before investing in a cold frame.

Really tender plants need to be brought inside for the winter. But not in an unheated garage. Besides, most garages don't have enough light. They need to spend the winter in the house. Many containerized plants are really houseplants that are taken outdoors in the warm weather but brought indoors when it gets cold.

When deciding on how you're going to insulate your containerized plants, consider the amount of work necessary and whether you can handle it by yourself or whether you should enlist the help of family, friends or your gardener.

It's all about doing what's best for you and your plants. As you can see, there are a number of choices to fit everyone's capabilities.

ONE MORE TASK: MULCH FOR WINTER

An extra layer of mulch in your planting beds and around your trees and shrubs is like putting a scarf around them for the winter. Arborists and landscapers recommend two or three inches of mulch during the growing season and up to four inches of mulch for the winter in cold climates. Of course, that's too much mulch for warmer climates.

I prefer organic mulch like wood chips. As they decompose, the wood chips add organic matter to the soil. Organic mulch moderates the soil temperature, reducing the effects of extreme cold or unseasonable warmth. It also absorbs some of the water from winter rains and melting snow so as not to drown the plants. It then releases the water in a more controlled manner for the plants to use over time.

Mulch can be purchased in big bags at your garden center or you can order it in bulk from a tree and landscape company. The latter is less expensive but they just dump it in your driveway.

Either acquisition method can be difficult for many seniors. You have to haul big bags of mulch to your planting beds, cut them open, dump them and spread the mulch. Or you have to shovel the mulch into a wheelbarrow or other conveyance, haul it to the planting bed, dump it and spread it.

This task can be tough on a senior's joints, muscles, heart and breathing. If you feel up to doing it yourself, consider investing in a two-wheel wheelbarrow or a garden wagon rather than trying to manage a single-wheel wheelbarrow. If you don't feel able to do the job don't push it. Enlist the help of your gardener, if you have one, or hire the landscaper from whom you buy the mulch to spread it for you.

Regardless of who spreads the mulch, be careful that it's not piled up against trunks and stems. Keep it an inch or two from the trunk or stem. Most of all, don't make mulch volcanoes by piling it up against the trunk or stem. Mulching right up against the trunk or stem provides timid rodents with just the camouflage they need to dine on your plants this winter.

One more caution: Next spring, return your beds to your normal summer mulch depth by removing the mulch that you add now.

SENIORS & SNOW – A DEADLY COMBO
OR JUST ANOTHER SEASON?

*H*ere's a question for senior gardeners who live in snowy northern climates: What do you do when the snow flies? Do you try to do the same shoveling or snow blowing that you did a decade or two ago? Or do you sit in your nice, warm house and let a plowing contractor take care of snow and ice removal? I hope it's the latter.

Every winter, we hear of seniors suffering heart attacks or falling and breaking bones in winter. Doing that can put a real crimp in your gardening activities next spring. Haven't we all earned the right to slow down and enjoy the winter scenery without having to go out and work in it?

The biggest concern most of us have is that nobody can plow as well as we can shovel or blow. Nobody will ever be able to do the job exactly as you would. However there is good news. Many good, reputable landscape contractors are now plowing snow in the winter. This is a good way for them to hang on to their talented, hard working employees through the winter.

When vetting contractors, check their qualifications. Ask if the person plowing your driveway does landscape or tree work in the summer. Be sure the contractor is fully insured with liability and worker's comp. Ask for references and then check them. Also check the home improvement websites like Angie's List, HomeAdvisors.com and the Better Business Bureau for an indication of the contractor's reputation.

When you've decided on a contractor, conduct an interview. Present the contractor(s) with a list of questions that you've printed out. Let the contractor know that you don't expect to find divots from the lawn in the middle of your yard and that you expect the contractor to replace any divots. Tell them where you want the snow piled. Be sure it isn't up against trees or shrubs like the ginkgo that's close to my driveway.

Ask them to shovel the walk to your front door and to de-ice wherever necessary, making sure that the de-icer doesn't ruin any plants. Some plow contractors don't like to leave their truck to do this. Scratch them off the list. Others may charge an extra fee, which is only fair.

Speaking of fees, most plow contractors offer a choice of payment methods. One method is a flat fee for the whole winter, the other is to pay for each plowing. It's a matter of which you feel most comfortable with. My significant other and I have the same contractor. She pays by the season and I pay by the plowing. If we have a lot of snowstorms, she saves money. If we have a mild winter, I make out better.

Regardless of how clean the pavement is, always walk as though you'll encounter black ice. If you use a cane, add a cleat. These just bolt on and can be flipped up out of the way when not needed. You can buy them at chain drug stores or medical supply stores. Even if you don't usually use a cane, you might consider a cleated cane for the winter. This isn't the time in your life for broken bones!

WINTERIZING YOUR EVERGREEN SHRUBS

Wrapping evergreen shrubs in burlap for the winter can be a chore as we grow older. Do you wrap because, "that's the way we've always done it." I'll bet it wasn't as strenuous when you were younger as it is now, though.

The fact is that only a small number of shrubs really need to be wrapped. They include young, tender plants that may be subject to road salt spray or are marginal for your hardiness zone. This doesn't mean that other evergreen shrubs don't need protection. It means that you can protect them with an antidesiccant material that's a lot easier than wrapping.

Antidesiccant is a wax-like material that you spray on the leaves and needles of your shrubs to reduce the chance of them drying out and branches dying over the winter. You can buy it in spray bottles at garden centers and apply it yourself. (The most common brand name is Wilt-Pruf.) Applying from spray bottles is fine if you only have a few shrubs to protect. But it can get very tiring if you have a lot of shrubs and trees to spray. If that's the case, it's more economical, as well as easier, to hire a tree or landscape company to apply it. They use a backpack sprayer with enough pressure to reach the tops of most evergreen trees.

While deciduous trees and shrubs go dormant when they lose their leaves, evergreens only "hibernate." Their bodily functions, including photosynthesis, continue, although at a much slower pace than during the growing season. Water, as well as sunlight, is needed for photosynthesis. During the growing season, the plants absorb water and nutrients from the soil. When the ground freezes in winter, the plants recycle the water they transpire through their leaves or needles as part of the reaction.

Winter winds can blow transpired water off the leaves or needles before it can be reabsorbed. As a result, the affected branches dry out and die, leaving brown spots in the foliage (See photo on previous page). Desiccation affects broadleaf evergreens like boxwood and rhododendrons even more than needled conifers because there is more leaf area. Antidesiccant holds the water on the leaf, where it can be reabsorbed as the plant needs it. I'd say that's pretty economical protection for your plants and for your body. I've used it for decades.

WINTER DOESN'T HAVE TO BE DRAB

*W*inter can be drab to say the least. It doesn't have to be, though. There are a few ways to add texture and even color to your property. It's important that you scale these ideas to the size of your property and your physical abilities.

Ornamental grasses are the workhorses of winter color. But they do require some work. The object is for the grass to give you four season interest. During the growing season, it grows tall and green. In late summer or early fall, seed heads develop interesting textures on top of the stalks or blades. The grass then turns a tanish color for the winter. When snow falls, the grass is still visible above the snow.

In spring, it has to be cut back almost to the ground to begin the process all over again. You have a choice of tools to do the cutting. Some people use hedge trimmers, others use string trimmers and still others use loppers. I don't recommend planting any more than you can comfortably take care of. I have a big patch of it in the back yard and clipping used to be a spring ritual. I'd then drag it up the hill and spread it around for mulch. I could never do that today. My gardener takes care of it now.

The photos above show two small clumps in the front yard – one in summer and one in winter. I could definitely cut them back with my geared hedge trimmers. But as long as the gardener is doing the back, he also does the front.

A few plants bloom in winter, with winter pansies being the most popular. Dogwood shrubs show off their colored branches in winter while holly plants display their red berries. Holly shrubs are dioecious, which means male and female flowers are on separate plants. So you need a male holly plant nearby to have red berries on the female plants. Monoecious plants have both flowers on a single plant.

If you typically cut back all of your herbaceous perennials, try leaving the tall ones to poke up through the snow. Brown seed heads break up the endless sea of white. Cutting back herbaceous perennials can then be crossed off your fall list without you ever having to raise a hand

In previous chapters, I've suggested replacing your woody perennials with shrubs. Shrubs, too, can add winter interest, especially evergreens. Some evergreens will hold snow on them, giving the garden interesting contours. Others will let most of the snow fall off the needles, giving you a classic winter scene.

I have two heavy, molded concrete statues in two of my gardens. When I was able to walk without a cane, I'd roll them onto a dolly and take them to storage in the garage. Then I had grandkids move them for a few years. Last winter, I simply wrapped them in clear trash bags and left them in place. One more way to add winter interest. Who said winter had to be drab and dull?

HOLIDAY GIFT IDEAS

As we get older, friends and family begin to think of us seniors as people who have everything, especially when it comes to holiday shopping. That may be because they ask what we want for Christmas and we can't come up with an answer.

If you're in the process of adapting your garden to your changing needs and capabilities, you should have plenty of gift ideas. How about one or more new, ergonomic tool(s)? Or a book on adaptive gardening? Or even a promise to help you make some adaptive modifications to your garden in the spring?

Your tool request should be specific or you'll have one more useless item taking up space in your garage or shed. Determine what ergonomic tools you need. If possible or feasible, visit a garden store that carries them and give them a test drive. Otherwise, check the garden supply companies online and see what's available. Then you can answer each person who asks with a specific tool.

If your current tools are too heavy, you may only need lighter weight versions like those with fiberglass handles. For arthritis, ask for light weight tools with larger diameter handles or a foam sleeve to give them the extra diameter without adding to the weight. If strength or arthritis is making cutting tools like pruners and loppers more difficult to operate, ask for a ratchet or geared model like those made by Fiskars.

Reading in front of the fireplace is a good way to spend a blustery winter evening. Two books that I always recommend are *Slow Gardening* by Felder Rushing and *Gardening for a Lifetime* by the late Sydney Eddison. I've read them several times and have adopted many of their ideas to my adaptive process. *Slow Gardening* isn't on adaptive gardening but is all about simplifying your garden, and gardening smarter. A new book, *The Lifelong Gardener: Garden With Ease and Joy At Any Age* by Toni Gattone, was published in August, and I just finished reading it.

You might ask each family member for one of these three books. If you have to choose just one, I recommend making your choice based on where you are in your adaptive journey at this time. Sydney Eddison chronicled the adaptations she is had to make as she grew older, including the thought process she went through to reach her decisions. Toni Gattone is in an earlier stage in her adaptive process and has some good ideas on how younger gardeners can plan ahead and design their gardens with future needs in mind. *Slow Gardening* is a fun read with some really good ideas for making gardening more enjoyable and less work.

A third idea – promises of help – involves asking each family member who asks for a gift idea to help you with a particularly difficult task during the upcoming gardening season. How you approach that depends entirely on your family dynamic, You'll have to figure out the tact you'll take on your own.

HAVE A SAFE & HAPPY HOLIDAY SEASON

When you prepare for the holidays, I hope you are considering your age when deciding how much preparation you can do and the way you approach it. Many holiday preparations share the same hazards as outdoor gardening. They've just moved indoors.

Most holiday decorations involve lifting heavy objects, descending and ascending stairs, climbing ladders and dealing with dangerous materials. Trying to do too much too fast can result in your happy holidays being less than happy. Hopefully, you'll be celebrating with family and friends, most of whom are younger and more able to take on the challenges that you can no longer accept. If you have no family to help, why not enlist the person who helps you in the garden during the growing season?

Most families store their decorations either in the basement or the attic. Lugging heavy or bulky boxes up or down stairs can be a strain on your back, legs or arms, and this can lead to slippage and falling down stairs. Such a fall may result in bumps and bruises for the young person you enlist to help. If you try it, though, it will most certainly lead to a trip to the ER to mend sprains and breaks. There go the happy holidays you so look forward to.

Once everything is where it's needed, there's no problem with you hanging decorations on the tree at your height and within your reach. Those that require a ladder or stool should be left to the youngsters. That includes such tasks as putting the angel on top of the tree, hanging mistletoe and any other job in which you have to leave the floor.

Most holiday traditions include candles in their celebrations. At holiday time, fire departments see an upturn in house fires, and many of them are caused by candles. Besides the candle hazards that apply to everyone, there are others that we should be aware of as we age

As we age, we may forget to extinguish candles before going to bed. I've solved this problem by substituting electric candles for the traditional ones. These include little tea candles (see bottom photo below) that look surprisingly real without giving off any heat.

Finally, be careful when walking outside during the holiday season. Falling on ice can make for a very unhappy holiday season. Follow these tips and have a wonderful holiday season.

When Outdoor Gardening Is Out Of The Question

THE HOUSEPLANT REVOLUTION
GARDENING'S NEWEST TREND

Since starting the Geriatric Gardener in 2017, I've observed a number of trends begun by senior gardeners that are now embraced by young adults. And guess who gets the credit. Spoiler alert: It's not us senior gardeners.

The latest trend is an explosion of interest in houseplants. Houseplants have always been a popular alternative for senior gardeners who have downsized to apartments, condos or senior living facilities, or for whom working outside is too difficult. Today, younger generations are opting for urban living in which their opportunities to garden are restricted. This living choice is also influenced by college debt, time constraints and lack of interest in suburban living.

We seniors just gravitated to growing houseplants as either an extension of our outdoor gardening or as a necessary substitute for outdoor gardening. We are well aware of plants' ability to clean the air, reduce stress and bring a bit of nature indoors. Young people who began embracing houseplants turned to the internet to learn more about choosing the best plants and how to care for them. They even call themselves "Plant Parents," and there is a company by that name that offers plant care services when owners are away.

I've hired out nearly all of my outdoor garden maintenance and have concentrated on houseplants. Through on-the-job experience, I've become quite a fan of Tillandsias (air plants). I don't know whether I'm setting any trends but my collection is growing, mostly from offshoots, and I'm happy as a clam since air plants are so easy to care for.

My first alert to this houseplant phenomenon was an item in Dr. Allan Armtage's e-newsletter. Dr. A is a retired horticulture professor who is now a writer and consultant to the green industry. Then I read a story about new trends on a trade magazine's website, and realized that, once again, we senior gardeners were trend setters and didn't even realize it. So, let's just have fun with our houseplants and other gardening ideas and let others take credit when they finally catch up.

YOUR INDOOR GARDEN

*H*ow many plants live IN your house? Together, these make up your indoor garden,
and they need your TLC just as much as your
outdoor garden does.

As you age and turn more and more of your
outside gardening over to your helper(s), your
itchy green thumb can be satisfied by caring
for your indoor garden. This will become even
more important if you have problems breathing in very hot summer
temperatures. Retreating indoors will be your healthiest decision.

I'm at the stage now where I've turned almost all of my outdoor gardening over to others. Although I don't have breathing problems, I'm not
going to go out, lean on my cane and supervise what these professionals
are doing. So, I stay inside and tend to my indoor garden.

At last count, I had 62 indoor plants. I found that I give them too much
care rather than too little. Over caring, especially giving them too much
water and fertilizer, is worse than too little. Many of my indoor plants
are succulents and I've drowned a few with love.

Now, I'm into a routine. Once every other week is plant watering day.
I begin by immersing my air plants in water for at least an hour. While
they're soaking, I check all the potted plants with a moisture meter and
water only those that need it.

Don't be concerned if your indoor plants have looked a little disoriented
and appear to have the seasons backwards. I have no proof but it makes
sense if they do. We keep our houses warm in the winter and cool in the
summer, don't we? That's just the opposite of the outdoor climate. Although the temperatures are reversed, seasonal light changes are normal,
so you can see how your houseplants can be a bit neurotic. Controlling
the climate and the amount of light plants receive in a greenhouse is
how horticulturists force plants to flower out of season for spring flower
shows.

While indoor gardening may not provide the same amount of satisfaction as outdoor gardening, it's still very satisfying and keeps my green
thumbs from turning blue. If you're not into indoor gardening now, give
it a try. You might open up a whole new gardening adventure when you
thought adventures had become history.

AIR PLANTS
A WHOLE NEW GARDENING EXPERIENCE

Air plants are, arguably, the easiest, most low maintenance plants to grow. You don't even have to get your hands dirty since they don't grow in potting mix. Rather, they absorb air, water and nutrients through their leaves and roots.

More than 600 species of air plants, not including varieties or cultivars,. have been identified in the genus Tillandsia, which belongs to the Bromiliad family. The Spanish moss that you see growing on trees in the south is also a member of the Tillandsia genus and all of them are epiphytes. This means they can grow on another plant or some inanimate object but are not parasites. Rather they are sustained by the water and air that they absorb through their leaves and roots.

Most air plants are from Central America. Others are grown in Mexico, South America and even the southern United States. They are sold at many garden stores and even at festivals and fairs

The ways that air plants can be displayed are limited only by your imagination. Mine live indoors and rest either in the tops of flower vases or in pots filled with small stones or peat moss pads. At the other extreme is a senior citizen in Florida who mounts them on the trees in his yard.

The photos show the various ways that I display them. Those pictured above live in the holes in a piece of cactus wood. The single plant in the little clay pot on the next page is simply standing up in pebbles. The two plants next to it are standing in little pots lined with peat moss. This array includes my first air plant. It's the big one standing upright in the pot. Those in the big array are simply lying on pebbles and those on the windowsill are standing in the neck of a vase.

These plants need very little care – only watering and an occasional fertilization. Some "experts" advocate misting air plants every day. Other will tell you to submerge them in a bucket of water for at least an hour every few weeks. The grower in Florida depends entirely on the rain to water his. When I first started growing air plants, I misted them but now I submerse them for at least an hour every two weeks and they are growing just fine.

Air plants may not need watering often but they do need water. A teenage grandchild became intrigued with my air plants and asked if they were easy to grow. So, we went to our local garden store and bought her some. She must have interpreted infrequent watering as never because she managed to kill them.

Some people like to add fertilizer to the water but I'm not a big houseplant fertilizer person. When I think of it I put houseplant fertilizer in the submersion water once in the spring and once in the summer. However, they do need light, and prefer indirect sunlight.

They do reproduce by seed, but they also sprout pups, or offsets, that you can disconnect from the parent and, thus, expand your collection. I started with two from a festival about 20 years ago. One died, the other is still thriving. Over the years, I may have bought or received a half dozen more as gifts. The rest of my 20 were pups from the other plants.

Growing air plants wasn't on my bucket list. I saw them at a fair or festival several decades ago and I bought a couple from the vendor, and still have one of the original plants. Most are pups that I separated from mother plants. Today, I have about 20.

After growing air plants for years, I finally read a book on the subject in about 2014. The book I chose was *Air Plants – The Curious World of Tillandsias* by Zenaida Sengo. I read the book cover-to-cover. When leaves turned brown after some of my plants flowered, I was concerned that they would die as some succulents do after flowering. So, I emailed Ms.  Sengo and she assured me that they would bounce back, and they did.

As you continue to age and tasks you like to do continue to get more difficult, you'll appreciate Tillandsia's ease of maintenance. I recently had to use the newspaper on the kitchen table technique to repot some traditional plants that had outgrown their previous containers. You can probably picture the mess without further description. Not a problem with air plants. And imagine the look on unsuspecting friends' faces when you tell them that those lush, green plants don't have any soil under them.

Many gardeners, myself included, were introduced to air plants at farmer's markets or local arts & crafts festivals. We then sought out air plants at better garden centers in our communities. One garden center in our small town sells them and there are many more garden centers selling them in our metro area. So, finding air plants in your community shouldn't be a problem.

Have fun and enjoy your clean fingernails.